STOP PUSHING: I'M ALREADY DEPRESSED

CONQUERING DEPRESSION AND REDISCOVERING HAPPINESS

KEVIN BOYD

t

"Cover design by Getcovers"

CONTENTS

Introduction   5

1. J - JUMP-START YOUR JOURNEY   11
   Know Thy Enemy   13
   Causes   15
   Impact of Depression   18
   Unveiling the Truth – Debunking Depression Myths   22
   Pause and Ponder   24
   Segue   25

2. O - OPEN UP TO NEW APPROACHES   27
   A New Frontier – Exploring Novel Methods   28
   Shrooms   29
   Esketamine   30
   Virtual Reality   31
   Biofeedback   32
   Light Therapy   34
   Art and Music   36
   Pet Therapy   38
   Flotation Therapy   40
   Nutritional Psychiatry   41
   Digital Detox and Nature Therapy   43
   Yoga Nidra   46
   Pause and Ponder   49
   Segue   49

3. U - UNDERSTAND YOUR DEMONS   51
   What Do You Know?   51
   Why Self-Awareness Is Essential in Understanding
   Depression   52
   Tools for Self-Assessment   54
   Recognizing Triggers   55
   The Power of Journaling   59
   Exercises in Self-Reflection   63
   Pause and Ponder   64
   Segue   64

4. R - RECLAIM CONTROL   65
   Mindfulness and Relaxation Techniques   65
   Cognitive Behavioral Therapy (C.B.T.) Basics   71
   Coping Mechanisms – Sorting the Effective From
   the Ineffective   74
   Pause and Ponder   77
   Segue   78

5. N - NURTURE HOPE AND POSITIVITY   81
   The Science of Happiness   81
   Finding Joy Amid the Gray   83
   The Potential of Optimism   88
   Triumph Over Adversity: Inspiring Stories   91
   Mindset Matters: The Psychological Angle   94
   Daily Habits of Positivity   95
   Pause and Ponder   96
   Segue   99

6. E - EMBRACE LONG-TERM HEALING   101
   Sustaining Progress With Long-Term Strategies   102
   The Role of Gratitude   103
   Recognizing When to Seek Professional Help   106
   Preparing for Life's Ups and Downs   107
   Strengthening Social Connections   110
   Pause and Ponder   114
   Segue   114

7. Y- YIELD ENDURING CHANGE   115
   The Positive Aspects of Change   115
   Finding Comfort in Uncertainty   117
   Cultivating Habits for Lasting Change   119
   Pause and Ponder   123
   Segue   126

   Conclusion   129
   References   133

INTRODUCTION

THE INNER WAR

Depression feels like you're at war with yourself every moment of every day. You feel misunderstood and alone, even when your loved ones show they care. You know you shouldn't feel this way, but you have no control over the intrusive thoughts that invade your mind night and day. They bubble up inside you and won't go away no matter what you try. You either sleep too much or can't sleep at all. Either way, you're exhausted all the time. You can't concentrate, and you either lose or gain weight. Your confidence is shot, and you just don't feel well.

I've been there and sometimes still struggle with it myself. I've tried everything: therapists, medication, the works. While these methods are great for some, I realized they were only bandages that wore off after a while. What I needed was a treatment plan that had a permanent impact on my mental health. I found the J.O.U.R.N.E.Y. method the most profoundly life-changing technique ever. I felt that I had to share it with the world, hoping it would also improve your lives.

Starting Your J.O.U.R.N.E.Y.

J.O.U.R.N.E.Y. is an anagram that frames the techniques you can apply to your daily life. Each chapter features the following letter, the next step, to guide your journey to mental wellness. I will show you how to incorporate traditional therapies (like cognitive behavioral therapy) with more unconventional ones (like virtual reality) for a comprehensive program that works. A wide variety of methods make it easy to choose those that appeal to you so you have an individualized plan of action to deal with your depression. For the J.O.U.R.N.E.Y. framework, you will:

- Jump-start your journey
- Open up to new approaches
- Understand your depression
- Reclaim control
- Nurture hope and positivity
- Embrace long-term healing
- Yield to enduring change

You are a unique person. Although many suffer from depression, we each suffer differently. There is no single reason for depression, and there is no single way to deal with it. I give you choices to suit your needs within the J.O.U.R.N.E.Y. structure that gives you both freedom and security, ensuring you don't get too overwhelmed to take the next step.

Cloud Busting

I had the most trouble talking to a therapist. I wasn't comfortable telling a stranger my problems. Even though it was their job, I felt they were judging me. Depression is more recognized today than ever before, but there is still this cloud of shame surrounding it.

"You just want attention."

"Why can't you just get over it?"

"Well, you're dramatic."

I know I've heard these things more than once. You probably have, too. Even well-meaning friends and family may slip with phrases like these. They claim they're trying to help, but instead, the opposite occurs. You believe your feelings don't matter and are discouraged from speaking up. Your confidence dwindles as your depression grows. I'll tell you a secret about those helpful phrases. Depression doesn't work that way. People who have experienced it would never say something like that. Someone not understanding your pain doesn't invalidate it.

Depression does not make you strange, different, or an outcast. According to the World Health Organization, about 3.8 percent of the population is going through depression (WHO, 2023). That's about 280 million people. There is no reason for the unspoken shame surrounding it in our modern world. We are more globally connected, educated, and advanced than ever. It's time to stop treating this problem with superstition. It's an illness, plain and simple. Like any other illness, treatments must be tried until you find one that works for you. You can't be treated if you're ashamed to ask for help.

The first step to busting the cloud of shame is to know what depression is and its common misconceptions. The average person may think they know, but those are only assumptions unless they have been studied in detail. I will help you gain a deeper understanding by separating the facts and myths in a way that's easy to understand.

My goal is to give you a practical guide with approachable steps to take control of your mental health. Clear strategies for understanding and success are essential for taking care of yourself. Focus is difficult when depression hits, and a book full of nonsensical medical jargon won't help. I offer understandable explanations and actions you can take immediately for self-empowerment. You'll learn how to manage your symptoms and relieve your distress quickly.

No matter what stage your depression is in, this book offers you encouragement and hope. You can take control of your mental health without judgment or shame, and I can help bring clarity to your illness.

Not Just a Bandage

If you're looking for a long-term plan to manage your depression symptoms, this is the book for you. It's designed for overall mental health maintenance instead of a temporary fix. Of course, there are techniques to help ease your pain immediately, but the goal is everlasting happiness. You will learn how to develop your resilience, making it easier to bounce back from a depressive episode. You will learn to build your social circle and understand how important social support is. When depression strikes, it seems easier to isolate yourself. Part of the illness is feeling like nobody understands (or cares), even when you have loved ones who do. This is a trick, and reaching out is more important than ever.

GREGG'S STORY

In his early twenties, Gregg lived in the most exciting city in the world. Dubbed "the city that never sleeps," it lived up to its name. There were millions of people and constant activity, but Gregg felt more isolated each day. He used to be a passionate student with big dreams of making a difference in the world. Slowly, the passion died, and he struggled to find that sense of purpose that drove him. The days bled into one another, and he was going through the motions, lost in the fog that depression had surrounded him with.

He tried to escape the inner torment of his mind by going for walks and immersing himself in art and music. He enjoyed the peaceful bliss of nature, and his creativity quieted the constant chatter in his head. However, these moments didn't last, and he found himself losing interest. Once again, he was going through the motions, hoping to get the peace back. He felt disconnected from the entire world, and the hopelessness seeped back in.

Gregg started a journal to process his emotions at his therapist's suggestion. He discovered that it was easier to write what he found difficult to say out loud, even to the therapist. He wasn't ready to let someone in, so he told the bare minimum in his sessions and saved the deep emotions for his journal.

Everything changed when he was on one of his walks. He passed by a small art gallery and decided to go in. The gallery featured work by different artists that highlighted mental health issues. He could tell they struggled like him as each piece moved him with the raw emotion it unleashed. He felt the struggle, despair, and recovery that every brushstroke conveyed. Every sculpture took his breath away, and he could see the love and sadness worked into it. For the first time in what seemed like forever, Gregg felt seen.

His connection to the world around him was coming back, and the fog of depression began to dissipate. These artists knew exactly what he was going through, and it gave him hope.

This inspired him so much that he decided to create his own art. Sketches, paintings, and digital art gave him the catharsis he needed more than talking ever did.

Although he still struggled with his depression, Gregg found renewed life and purpose. This allowed him to manage his symptoms better. His art helped him build new friendships and mend old ones. He displayed his work in the same gallery to inspire others who suffer from depression as he had been inspired.

Gregg's story is not one of a miracle cure but a process of recovery. The nagging doubts, fears, and despair cannot be banished, but you can accumulate moments of peace until they override your depression. Don't be too proud to seek help and find outlets that bring you joy. Your solution may look different than Gregg's, but it *is* yours.

INSPIRATION AND HOPE

That is my wish for anyone who decides to pick up this book. I want to bring you inspiration and hope with the J.O.U.R.N.E.Y. framework like Gregg found in the art gallery. It has helped me so much with my depression that I would be selfish if I didn't share.

J - JUMP-START YOUR JOURNEY

> *"That's the thing about depression: A human being can survive almost anything as long as she sees the end in sight. But depression is so insidious, and it compounds daily, that it's impossible to ever see the end."*
>
> — ELIZABETH WURTZEL

There are countless ideas on what depression is and isn't. I will start by clearing that up for you so you can better understand your condition. Only when you truly know what you're up against can you fight it confidently. Sometimes, it's set off by a traumatic event. Sometimes, it creeps up on you out of nowhere. Sometimes, it hits suddenly. Other times, it sneaks in so gradually that you don't notice until it's too late.

Caleb used to be energetic and driven, but now all he could do was stare at a book, and he hadn't turned a page in hours. He heard the bustle of city traffic outside his window and heard people walking dogs and saying "hi" to the neighbors, but it seemed so far away.

His mind was a hurricane that wouldn't die, but he couldn't physically move. All of his racing thoughts centered around the biggest shock of his life. His sister Ava was going into renal failure. It was advanced enough that there was nothing they could do. She had always been healthy and active. The news was too much for Caleb and the rest of his family to bear.

Depression dug into his soul as the house that used to carry so much laughter grew silent. Ava was the one who held everyone together. She planned events, hosted the dinners, and spread joy wherever she went. Now, the family took turns caring for her in quiet resignation. They were all helpless, and Caleb felt its weight as he could only watch his family suffer. It was as if some cruel game master had taken over, and there was nothing he could do as they were pushed around like chess pieces. Hope was fading with his sister's life; the only joy he could find was in their shared childhood memories.

His friends and loved ones checked in on him, trying to connect, but he couldn't reciprocate. He wanted to with all his heart, but the depression had paralyzed him. He was between not wanting to burden anybody (they had enough to worry about with Ava) and feeling like they couldn't possibly understand. He couldn't fathom living without his sister and mourned the person she used to be.

As he sat alone in his dark and silent room, it struck him that depression had sunk its teeth into him. With that came the realization that the rest of the family must feel the same way. The problem was more significant than him, and he was too involved in his despair to consider their feelings. This unseen enemy preyed on their weaknesses and infiltrated their minds.

That realization made him angry, and the anger sparked a bit of hope. He vowed to be strong enough to fight to stand by Ava in her time of need. His task was to pull the family together and inspire hope in them.

He knew he had a long way to go. His journey was beginning, and it would take work. He swore that he would find the light in dark times. He would create it if he had to—for his parents, Ava, and himself.

KNOW THY ENEMY

Caleb's experience highlights how depression can have an impact not only on you but also on those who care about you the most. Although you may not realize it, your loved ones care deeply about you and want nothing more than to help you. However, the first step towards recovery is to help yourself by learning about the illness and how to fight it.

The most evident symptom of depression is an intense feeling of sadness. It's not just a minor feeling but a deep, uncontrollable sadness that can eat away at you from within, leaving you empty and hopeless. You may find yourself crying involuntarily at the worst possible moments, and it can become debilitating if left unchecked.

Another less obvious symptom of depression is irritability. You may find yourself becoming impatient and frustrated by even minor inconveniences. If left unchecked, this could lead to violent outbursts, which may manifest in various ways, such as yelling, throwing objects, or attacking others. However, if you recognize the signs of an oncoming episode, you can take steps to prevent it from escalating.

You may also lose interest in daily tasks and the things that used to bring you the most joy. You cancel plans more often; hobbies are left to collect dust, and you can forget about sex. That's not happening anytime soon. You've lost your drive to accomplish anything and ask yourself all too often, "What's the point?"

Your sleep patterns become unbalanced when depression hits. Either you've got insomnia, or you sleep too much. Generally, there is no happy medium. If you can't sleep, your mind races with intrusive negative thoughts that won't let up. When you sleep too much, your mind wants to shut everything down, and even when you're awake, it's a fight to focus on anything for more than a few seconds.

Even if you don't experience sleep disturbances, you may develop chronic fatigue. You're always tired and feel like you're moving through water. Most minor chores feel like construction work and simple things like brushing teeth require effort.

Your relationship with food may change when depression hits. Either your stomach is too nauseous to eat, or you binge food that's not good for you. Rapid losses or gains of weight are to be expected when you're going through a depressive episode.

Depression can cause restlessness and agitation. It becomes challenging to stay still for more than a few moments as your mind keeps returning to your problems. To cope with this, you may look for external distractions, making you feel jumpy and irritable when you can't find any.

You may find yourself dwelling on mistakes that you made long ago. Your brain won't let you forget that time when you were twelve and made your mom cry with harsh words. It would help if you had let that stranger have your seat on the bus ten years ago. Yesterday, everything seemed to go wrong, and you can't get over the feeling that you fail everything you try. Your mind will circle all the perceived mistakes you can remember, making them seem larger than they are.

All of the previous symptoms contribute to the inability to think straight. You have more trouble making decisions than you used to. You're either second-guessing yourself or don't know which choice is correct. Your loved ones may accuse you of not paying attention. The truth is, you need help remembering their words. You become spacey, and little details disappear. It would help to remember why you went into the kitchen, even though you have an empty water glass. You can't find your keys, but they're on their proper hook by the door.

You dwell on thoughts of suicide or death in general. Maybe you've already tried to commit suicide. This is a clear sign that you need help *now*. Please reach out by telling a friend or family member, calling a suicide prevention hotline, or calling emergency services. Help is out there if you're willing to accept it.

Depression can have physical consequences, too. Often, these are dismissed because you must have slept wrong for your back to ache the way it does. Maybe your uptick in headaches is due to allergies. Of course, you want any physical ailment checked out by a doctor, but if they can't tell why these things are happening, they could be the result of depression (Sawchuk, 2022).

CAUSES

This question can be complex as depression has many causes. Just to be clear, sadness is expected under the right circumstances. You're supposed to mourn the loss of a loved one. You're supposed to feel lonely at times. You feel the emotion and move on when the dust settles. If it lasts more than two weeks after that, then the sadness could be mutating into depression (Centers for Disease Control and Prevention, 2023). With clinical depression, the emotions run deeper and impact your way of life. They destroy your routines and the way you care for yourself and others.

Genetics do play a role in the onset of depression. If your family has a history of the illness, you could also be at risk. If it hasn't happened yet, becoming familiar with the symptoms listed previously will go a long way in prevention. You can head it off at the pass, making its management much more accessible.

Chemical imbalance in the brain causes a variety of mental illnesses, including depression. When neurotransmitters and neurocircuits miscommunicate, your moods and thought patterns change. This condition requires a medical diagnosis and may necessitate treatment with corrective medication.

If your overall personality already leans toward melancholy, then you may be at risk for depression. There is a subculture of people who romanticize their negative emotions, and they fit into this category. Most are regular people who tend to see things on a darker slant. The "glass is half empty" folks.

Severe and chronic illness can lead to depression. As your physical health degrades, you can begin to dwell on all the things you did when you could and mourn that you can't anymore. The feelings of failure bubble up, and perhaps you feel you've become a burden to your family.

Many people tend to self-medicate with drugs and alcohol instead of reaching out to a qualified professional. The problem with this is that it only makes depression worse. Depression and addiction feed each other and almost always end at rock bottom.

Some people don't handle change very well, and it could result in depression. A lost job, moving, a car accident, or any number of things can turn your life upside down. Adapting to new circumstances can make positive life events, such as getting married, trigger depression.

This list can be overwhelming, but everything on it is treatable. Happiness can be yours again if you put in the work.

Joe's Journey

Joe fought to keep his job, but due to company-wide cutbacks, he was laid off. He was divorced and could only visit his two kids every other weekend. He held onto his house as long as he could, but eventually, the bank foreclosed on it. He was out looking for work every day, but nothing panned out. A friend offered him a camper while he got back on his feet.

He knew depression was sinking in when he went on his job hunt less often. He felt at a loss, as his options were limited where he was. He found getting up in the morning more challenging, as he had to drive daily from his friend's camper on the city's outskirts. He canceled visitation with his kids because he didn't want them to see him as a failure.

One day, his friend, Jeremy, came to check on him. It was late afternoon, and Joe was still in bed. The camper was a mess of fast food wrappers and dirty clothes. He braced himself, expecting to be kicked out. Instead, his friend patiently waited for him to sit up before sitting beside him. He looked concerned, not angry. That inspired Joe to truly listen to what he had to say.

Jeremy didn't berate or judge Joe. Instead, he recognized that Joe was sinking. Having been through something similar, Jeremy truly sympathized. He worried about Joe's decline and suggested he talk to someone. Jeremy asked him if he ever thought about ending it all. He never actively considered it but had to admit that it had been lurking in his mind. It was then that he realized Jeremy was right. He had to make an effort.

He got off the bed and started cleaning. Jeremy helped while listening to Joe's most profound thoughts. Joe didn't realize that what he needed was a sympathetic ear. He could think clearly for the first time in months. Jeremy left the camper, promising that Joe would start fresh in the morning.

Instead of another fruitless job hunt, Joe went to the city's mental health clinic. He found a therapist he could trust and inspiration to try a new line of work. The healing process had truly begun, and he now viewed himself as doing the best he could instead of a failure. He started visiting his kids and letting them inspire him to keep trying.

The struggle to return to everyday life was beginning, so he decided to treat it as an adventure for his children's sake.

IMPACT OF DEPRESSION

Depression takes a toll on your overall health. Please don't assume that it's all in your head. There are real medical repercussions when you suffer from depression.

Body

Depression isn't just an emotional condition. It's an actual illness with a physical impact on your body. You could experience headaches, fatigue, chronic pain, and eating disorders. If you develop an eating disorder, it could lead to malnutrition or diabetes (Pietrangelo, 2022). It's doubly important to eat as healthy as possible when depression hits.

The impact that chronic pain makes on your body is twofold; you feel the pain that's caused by the depression, yet the pain can make the depression worse. It cycles, magnifying each time until you get help for both your physical and mental health.

The fatigue caused by depression makes every effort you put in seem like moving a mountain. It becomes too challenging to shower, going to the grocery store makes your stomach knot up, and checking in with your friends and loved ones is exhausting. Soon, your hygiene is abysmal, and your friends haven't heard from you in weeks.

You're also at risk for heart problems. Depression increases your stress levels, and that increases your heart rate, putting your body into a state of hypervigilance. This increases the strain on your heart, which raises the risk of developing high blood pressure and heart disease.

Autoimmune conditions are a typical result of depression, although there is some debate on which causes which (Villines, 2023). What is known is that those who suffer from depression are also at risk for diseases like fibromyalgia and arthritis.

You can also experience stomach problems. Increased stress means increased stomach acid that wears down your entire gastrointestinal tract. You'll experience heartburn, ulcers, and bowel issues.

Mental Health

Depression is a multidimensional illness that impacts many areas of your mental health. Each is connected, culminating in a domino effect only you can see.

Depression changes the brain's physiology, leading to swelling or shrinking. The pressure these conditions put on the brain affects its primary functions: clarity, focus, memory, impulses, and even depth perception. These are vital for a healthy body (Wilson, 2018).

As your brain starts to change, the chemicals that regulate it decrease in production. Norepinephrine, serotonin, and dopamine act as apps for your brain, telling them what to do and how to react. With them producing as well as they should, you can avoid responding poorly to situations, forgetting things more frequently, and doing things on impulse that you usually wouldn't do (such as binge shopping).

Cortisol is the stress hormone that gets pumped through your system in force when you're going through a depressive episode. It's been suggested that the overabundance of this hormone can lead to chemical imbalances that change your brain (Solis-Moreira, 2023).

Have you realized that you need to handle change better than you used to? You can't understand a new idea. You can't grasp an innovative way to perform a task. It goes right over your head, but it's not your fault. A healthy production of chemicals ensures that your brain can learn and process new things. It automatically sets aside stuff it doesn't need to make room for new information and retains everything you use. When the chemicals fail, it can no longer do its self-maintenance.

You can see that it's not just your emotions that are depressed but also your bodily functions. "This can seriously impact your quality of life and worsen your emotional state of depression."

Social Interactions

There are plenty of people who are socially awkward and maybe even reclusive. That doesn't mean they are depressed. What you want to look for is a change in social behavior. If you were active just a couple of months ago, eager to make plans anytime you had off from work, and now you cancel plans; If you were a weekend warrior who spent all of your free time in nature, but now you don't have the time to do anything but sleep, you could be suffering from depression.

It would help if you consciously tried remaining active when troubled. If you don't, you'll find it all too easy to disappear into your blanket, never to be heard from again. Your friends and loved ones miss you, and you will miss them. You'll feel like you just bring them down when you're present, but that is your depression talking. Remember, you're not a mind reader, so you can't possibly know what they think of you unless they voice it.

Pushing people you love the most away is a tactic for you to disengage with life. Depression can seem like a separate living being, trying to divide you and your loved ones so it can have you all to itself. To keep this from happening, say yes more than you would like. You don't have to accept every invitation but show them you're making an effort. Be the one to make the plans once in a while. It shows that you are committed to the relationship and value their support. If you feel like you're sinking, ask them for help. They love you and will sympathize (Cassata, 2021).

UNVEILING THE TRUTH – DEBUNKING DEPRESSION MYTHS

It's human nature to jump to conclusions as part of our reasoning skills. It's how we advance our thinking abilities and learn new things. The problem is that most jump to a conclusion and assume it's fact. Without proof to back it up, it's still only an assumption. I want to separate fact from fiction to rid you of some of the confusion.

It Could Never Happen to Me

Depression is common and can happen to anyone. About 280 million people suffer from it, and women are at a higher risk than men (World Health Organization, 2023). Since various factors contribute to this illness, the best action is to be well-informed and prepared.

Even faces you see on television and social media have been open about experiencing depression. The most notable one at the moment was Robin Williams, famous for his ability to make the world laugh. He tragically took his own life in 2014 and is still mourned by his fans. Jim Carrey, another great comedian, has talked extensively about his depression. Country music star Naomi Judd wrote about her battle with depression in her book *River of Time: My Descent Into Depression and How I Emerged With Hope* (WebMD, 2012).

You are not immune to depression, nor are you alone in the struggle.

Depression and Sadness Are the Same Thing

Sadness is a normal emotion. Depression is an illness that has many symptoms, including perpetual sadness. Other symptoms are loss of interest in regular activities, appetite changes, pain and inflammation, feelings of failure, isolation and loneliness, and a decline in critical thinking.

Only the Weak Are Afflicted

You can't force depression to go away, just as you can't force diabetes away. Depression needs treatment, and ignoring it will only make it worse. The chemicals in your brain must be balanced, and strength of will has nothing to do with it.

You Can Wait It Out

I'm sorry, but it doesn't work that way. As a medical illness, depression must be acknowledged and treated. It does not go away without any effort on your part.

There Are No Treatments for It

As I said in the last myth, a medical illness must be treated. Many methods exist to achieve happiness, including psychotherapy and medication, meditation and affirmations, virtual reality, and creative visualization. It helps to keep your routines and social engagements, no matter how much you don't want to.

Meds Are the Only Option

Depression must be treated on a case-by-case basis. Some patients respond best with medication, and some respond better with therapeutic techniques. You and your doctor should collaborate to find the best treatment plan. If it's your first time, this may take some experimentation, but it will become easier once you find the best solution.

Talking About It Makes It Worse

This misconception arises from fear: people believe that if they verbalize their fears, they will become a reality. It's real now. It's not going away by itself. Many people have found that talking to a therapist helps them understand their condition and themselves. They can help you brainstorm ideas when you're at a loss. Sometimes, you need a sympathetic listener to work through all the chaotic negativity in your head. Give it a shot. You won't know if it works if you don't try it at least once.

You're Just Lazy

People in your social circle may not understand what you're going through. They may tell you you're lazy, inattentive, and don't need a doctor; you must get up and do something. Lack of interest is most definitely a symptom of depression, especially when it's a change from your usual pattern of behavior.

These assumptions are why you need to carefully consider your symptoms and talk to a qualified mental health professional.

PAUSE AND PONDER

These exercises are meant to get to know your symptoms and how you can begin your J.O.U.R.N.E.Y. back to happiness.

Reflect on Myth vs. Reality

Before reading this chapter, were there any myths you believed to be facts? How have your beliefs changed?

Personal Connection

Is there a time when you felt misunderstood in your struggle with depression? How did that make you feel? How can you use the insights for this chapter to communicate your experiences better?

Science Simplified

In your own words, summarize the basic scientific explanation of depression provided in this chapter. How does this knowledge empower your journey?

SEGUE

The next chapter is the next step of your J.O.U.R.N.E.Y.: Open up to new approaches. You'll discover novel ways to treat your symptoms for better mental health.

O - OPEN UP TO NEW APPROACHES

Y ou can try many less conventional techniques if you are open to them. If your old routines are not relieving you, it's time to branch out and discover new ways to find happiness.

Kaylee had been fighting major depression for years. She'd done everything she thought she should, but it was still a struggle. She'd been faithfully seeing her therapist once a month, tried psychotherapy and medication, went to yoga class, and developed a daily gratitude practice. All of these things did help, but she never found true happiness. She became skilled at masking her depression symptoms, but they were still like shadows in the back of her mind, waiting to engulf her the first chance they got. She was ready to try something new to boost her process of recovery.

Her therapist suggested getting a pet. Kaylee had never considered having one before. She wasn't allowed them as a child, and she felt insecure about caring for one now that she was grown. As a single woman with no children, her life was about work, and she didn't have room for much else. Her therapist talked her into it by suggesting that caring for something so dependent could be just what she needed.

Kaylee adopted an older cat instead of a kitten. She thought that it wouldn't be as needy as training a kitten. She was wrong. The two-year-old calico was lovely and needy. She wanted to cuddle constantly and pouted when she didn't get her way. Kaylee named her Honey Bun.

Playtime was the highlight of Honey Bun's day. Kaylee first saw it as a chore distracting her from being productive, but it only took a couple of weeks before it became the highlight. Honey Bun was too cute for words as she went after the toys, and the pure joy on her face was contagious. Kaylee felt joy as she watched her new baby chase and pounce those catnip-filled toys.

It happened gradually, so it was a while before she realized her spirits were lifted. Her therapy sessions were filled with happy chatter about Honey Bun. The therapist smiled like a proud mother the day she confessed she looked forward to inviting friends over for dinner. She no longer dreaded going to work in the morning because she had Honey Bun to come home to.

She wasn't ready for a romance yet, but thanks to Honey Bun, her heart was open, and she was prepared to rejoin the world.

A NEW FRONTIER – EXPLORING NOVEL METHODS

Kaylee's story shows that happiness can come from unexpected sources. Although you may be reluctant to try something new initially, you may be pleasantly surprised by the results.

An article from Q.P.S. states (2022):

Suicide is the second leading cause of death among Americans between the ages of 10 and 34, per the Centers for Disease Control and Prevention (C.D.C.). That alarming statistic is enough to classify suicide as a significant public health concern, even with the ubiquity of anti-depression drugs in today's pharmaceutical market. Fortunately, clinical researchers are working to explore novel approaches to treating depression (p. 1).

Antidepressants aren't always the answer, as brain function is unpredictable. Something that worked last week could stop being effective, and the meds must be adjusted. For some, this is a never-ending cycle of treatment. This is why the National Institute of Mental Health (NIMH) has given out eight grants to research innovative treatments for depression and reduce the rates of suicide (Q.P.S., 2022).

The problem with the most common antidepressants on the market is that they're made to increase the serotonin production in your brain, but it can take two or more weeks to see a significant change. Your depression may even worsen while you wait. As your brain gets used to the drug, it adjusts itself, and that requires an adjustment in the medication. About 30 percent of people suffering from this tragic illness don't respond to this type of antidepressant (Rodriguez & Zorumski, 2023).

SHROOMS

More aptly, psilocybin is the compound from hallucination-inducing mushrooms. Trials are in the works to explore it as a viable treatment option for the treatment of major depressive disorder (M.D.D.), especially those resistant to other therapies.

ESKETAMINE

Research has shown the most promising results with the keta-mine-derived esketamine, which works through glutamate, another neurotransmitter chemical, instead of serotonin. This has shown promise in people resistant to other treatments, and the Food and Drug Administration (F.D.A.) has approved a nasal spray called Spravato. This is an option to try if the typical serotonin-boosting medication doesn't work for you.

It will take a bit of experimentation to find the treatments that work for you. A recommended therapist may not suit you, so you'll have to try another one that's more of what you want. Sometimes, people don't vibe on your level. You may be recommended a medication, but you need to get results. That doesn't mean that there's anything wrong with you or the drug. Tell your doctor, and likely, they'll try a different one until the right one is found. Your openness to change and experimentation will be critical to your mental wellness.

Medication alone is not a long-term cure for depression. If you're willing to try other methods to complement your treatment, you can develop a routine more suited to you as an individual. Creating an exercise plan will help increase your serotonin levels and flood your system with endorphins. Junk food is addictive and provides a sugar rush. Like a drug, eventually, that wears off, and you're left in a foul mood with low energy. A nutrition plan will help you steady your energy levels and brain function. Activities that help you lower your stress will drastically improve your symptoms. For some, this will be things like meditation and breathing exercises. For others, it could be a hobby like painting or crochet. A friend of mine discovered that a punching bag was just the thing he needed to release his emotions and get some exercise, so don't be afraid to try something outside of your standard practices (Smith, MA et al., 2019).

Virtual reality, biofeedback, light therapy, art and music, pet therapy, flotation therapy, nutritional psychiatry, digital detox and nature therapy, and yoga nidra are unconventional therapies that I found to be the most helpful. I am happy to share them in hopes that you will, too.

VIRTUAL REALITY

Virtual reality therapy (V.R.T.) as a treatment for depression is the perfect example of moving forward in the digital age. At one time, virtual reality was only considered in science fiction. The last few decades have seen it come to life, primarily in the gaming community. Now, medical professionals are taking advantage of everything these technological wonders offer.

Gaming and V.R. therapy have one thing in common - they transport the user into a digital world in 3D. V.R. therapy is used for mental health treatment in conjunction with a therapist, and it is effective for various conditions, including depression. One of the benefits of V.R. therapy is that it offers anonymity in group therapy. Presenting oneself with a virtual avatar makes patients feel less vulnerable and more likely to open up without fear of judgment from their peers.

A step up from teletherapy—a phone or video session—V.R.T. offers an immersive experience where you can see and touch everything around you while staying in an environment that makes you comfortable (Laurence, 2022).

V.R.T. for Depression

How can virtual reality specifically help those who suffer from depression? The virtual model of this technique makes it accessible to almost everyone. If you're sure you could benefit from group therapy but are disabled and housebound, V.R.T. can put you right in the room with everyone else. It creates an experience that activates your senses instead of watching on a screen. V.R.T. does not involve medication, so it can be used alongside any other treatment you may face. It can enhance your learning experiences, help you develop empathy and understanding, and address your fears by tailoring the experiences to your needs.

There are a few downsides to V.R.T. You have to have expensive equipment to access it, which will be almost impossible if you're on a tight budget. You'll also have to pay for internet access and possibly subscription fees. That may break even when cutting the cost of travel, so you would have to decide which path is better.

While technology is great, it has problems that could seriously affect treatment. The internet lags, your memory card freezes, and the headset freezes. These are typical issues for everyday use, no more than an inconvenience, but for a patient, they could be the difference between calm and crisis. We all hope technology will evolve beyond these issues one day, but they are an irritating fact of life.

BIOFEEDBACK

According to the Mayo Clinic (2023):

Biofeedback is a mind-body technique for controlling body functions such as heart rate, breathing patterns, perspiration, temperature, and muscle responses. During biofeedback, you're connected to electrical pads that help you obtain information about your body (p. 1).

Like V.R.T., biofeedback is noninvasive and can be used with other treatments. You'll be given various methods to stimulate the sensors: pictures, videos, movements, or recordings. The sensors provide the feedback, and your therapist can help decipher it. Since most of our functions are involuntary, we need to know what specific stressors affect the body. Biofeedback helps solve that puzzle and teaches you what helps and what makes it worse. You will learn what to do when you feel like you're spiraling and what to avoid to prevent it from happening again. Once you've been guided through the biofeedback, you can use the control methods that work for you anywhere.

How to Use Biofeedback for Depression

This advanced method is excellent for several things, but how can it help with depression? What can you gain from strapped with padded sensors that check your physical operations? By monitoring your reactions to pleasant and unpleasant stimuli, you will learn things like your personal triggers for a depressive episode and things that lift you when you feel one coming. Maybe you have a physical reaction, like a headache, before an episode hits you. You will learn more about the connection between your physical and mental well-being.

Biofeedback involves learning different practices to control your stress responses. These practices relieve anxiety, slow your pounding heart, and lift your spirits. Once you can do them on cue, you'll see a remarkable improvement in your quality of life.

I previously mentioned how the brain slows down and essentially "rewires" itself due to reduced necessary chemicals. With biofeedback, you can train your brain to improve memory, eliminate brain fog, and replenish its elasticity. You learn to keep it wired the right way. This type of control will boost your confidence and take away your feelings of helplessness when you're in the middle of a depressive episode.

How to Get Started With Biofeedback

This kind of advanced treatment can be overwhelming to think about. Where would you sign up for something like this? Start by discussing it with your current mental health professional. They can help you decide if it's a good option for you if it's offered in your area, as well as the steps to take for a referral. There aren't any known side effects, but they will know best if it's a good choice for you. You may get lucky, and your doctor offers it, saving you some travel money.

Money is another thing to discuss. How much would such a treatment cost? Would your insurance cover it? If you do have to travel, can you afford it? Many of us are on a strict budget and must consider every extra expense.

If you decide that biofeedback suits you, you'll undergo an initial evaluation to determine your base readings. You'll decide what you want to get out of the sessions and how to proceed from there. Any changes are determined from the initial readings as you progress. Sessions take 30 minutes to an hour (Sears, PT, 2012).

LIGHT THERAPY

Light therapy is the regulated use of a light box to treat conditions that a lack of sunlight could contribute to. It has been wildly successful in treating a form of major depressive disorder

(M.D.D.) with seasonal patterns known as seasonal affective disorder (S.A.D.). S.A.D. is prevalent in the fall and winter months when it gets dark sooner, and the sun rises later. Five percent of adults in the U.S. are afflicted with S.A.D., and light therapy is one of the best treatments for this form of depression (Cleveland Clinic, 2021).

To experience the benefits of the lightbox, you sit in front of it for about 30 minutes a day. It sets your internal clock and boosts serotonin and norepinephrine levels to improve mood. If you decide this is your route, be aware that not all light boxes are the same. The ones explicitly used for light therapy block out ultraviolet rays, but there are those used for other ailments (such as skin conditions) that emit a limited amount of ultraviolet light.

There are a few downsides to consider when considering light therapy. It can cause an upset stomach, headache, and eye pain. Specific prescriptions can cause light sensitivity; light treatment wouldn't be for you if you're on any of them.

Ruby's Story

Ruby had been diagnosed with S.A.D. before it was changed to M.D.D. with seasonal patterns. She took medication year-round for her depression, but come fall, her struggle was twice as hard. The days were gloomy, and the night came too early. Her loving family surrounded her, but she couldn't join their fun. She just wanted to sleep all the time and had to force herself to take care of her six kids. As soon as they were off to school, she was out of energy and would sit on the couch and scroll through her phone for hours.

One of her scrolling sessions led to a breakthrough. She happened on a website explaining light therapy and how it worked. It was like an epiphany. After discussing it with the doctor, she decided to try it. It worked wonders. She no longer had to force herself to be present in her family's lives; she was on a regular sleep schedule and had the energy to lead an everyday life.

ART AND MUSIC

Art and music have long been known for their cathartic effects. Both speak to your mind on a symbolic level, which the subconscious understands. Especially for those who have difficulty voicing their feelings, creative outlets like art and music allow them to express themselves.

Also known as expressive therapy, using creative outlets can help those with depression by nurturing mindfulness, confidence, and inner peace. You can bring thoughts, feelings, and memories to the surface that you didn't know you were hiding. While this may be uncomfortable initially, using the arts to get it out of yourself can be deeply healing. Like my friend, Gregg, you may find healing by sharing your story through art.

Music doesn't only mean composition. I can't play a single instrument, and I'm tone-deaf. I like to put in my earbuds and select a playlist that suits my mood. I'll play fast music for more energy and easy listening for a mellow disposition. What matters is that the music speaks to me in a way that words cannot. Let that be your emotional doorway if you play an instrument or sing. If you dance, let your dance release those unwanted feelings.

You don't have to be naturally talented to try any creative outlet. What matters is that you enjoy it, and it helps heal your soul.

Tammy's Story

Tammy always struggled to communicate with people, even those closest to her. Her childhood home didn't allow any display of emotions, and that continued into her adulthood. Whenever she got upset, she felt guilty and apologized excessively. She couldn't speak up for herself either. After struggling with depression, she finally opened up to her therapist and got diagnosed. Her therapist asked Tammy if there was any art she was interested in. Tammy was thrilled that someone finally asked her that. She had been in the photography club in high school but stopped after a while. Now, she spent all her time caring for others, which was exhausting. Her therapist suggested that she take up photography again and try to express her emotions through her pictures.

Tammy took a bunch of black-and-white photos to her next session. She was surprised at how effortless it was to talk about her feelings as she showed each picture to her therapist. From then on, she brought her photos to every session, and talking became much easier. She eagerly awaited each appointment, and her therapist helped her work through anything she had trouble with. Tammy never thought she would showcase her talent to the world, but she felt like a new person.

Where to Begin?

Do you start drawing, hoping for the best? No, that's like learning to swim by jumping in the ocean. You need a professional trained in expressive therapy to work with you. They will teach you how to use your creativity toward mental health. You may need to ask your current doctor to refer you to someone specializing in this field. As always, you should consider costs and insurance coverage so there aren't any unexpected expenses thrown at you.

What Should You Expect?

You've found a therapist you like who specializes in expressive therapy. Now what? Although art and music have been the focus of this book, there are several kinds of expressive therapy, and together, you and the therapist will decide what works best for you. The therapist may have you try different things during a session or concentrate on one technique. They will guide you through your emotions as you create, and the creation embodies those emotions.

PET THERAPY

Pet therapy can be an excellent addition to your treatment for depression. More than regular pets, therapy-trained animals offer care and support that humans sometimes can't. They don't have to understand what you're going through; they only want you to feel better. If you decide to try it, you will schedule sessions (usually 30 minutes, but it can vary) with a well-trained animal and their equally well-trained handler. The animals are typically cats or dogs, but horses and rabbits are popular, too.

Pet therapy is used for a wide range of healing. Many nursing homes and hospitals have volunteer programs to bring therapy pets to infirm patients. Some services that cater to the developmentally disabled have had success teaching the residents to ride and care for horses. Children with trouble making friends can be coaxed out of their shells by regular playdates with their therapy dog. Veterans who have post-traumatic stress disorder (PTSD) can gain clarity and calm with a fluffy cat purring on their chest (Giorgi, 2013).

Brody's Story

Brody was a single father caring for his developmentally disabled son, Matthew (Matty). Matty was ten years old and on the autism spectrum, withdrawn, and he had frequent meltdowns. Brody was diagnosed with M.D.D. shortly after his wife died when Matty was five. His medication and therapy weren't helping as much as they used to, and Matty made sure that he didn't have the time to care for himself properly. He loved his son with all his heart but was exhausted and at his wit's end.

Another parent at the learning center for autism spectrum disorder (A.S.D.) that Matty attended five days a week told him about a nonprofit stable that catered to the developmentally disabled. He called them right away and set up an appointment. Matty resisted at first. He had never seen a horse before and had a screaming meltdown. Brody was afraid it would spook the horse, so he scooped up his boy and tried to calm him. The horse wasn't spooked at all. With her trainer at the reins, the horse slowly approached. If a horse could tiptoe, that's how it would look. She neighed softly and nuzzled Matty. To Brody's delight, Matty stopped crying and touched her nose.

Brody immediately felt some of his long-term despair fall away. It was several weeks before Matty was ready to ride Ginger, but by then, they had formed a bond that made Brody wish he could buy her. Brody shared Matty's joy when it was time to go to the stable. By the time Matty was 13, he was an expert rider and became communicative enough to volunteer once a month to help others like him. Brody would still struggle with grief and depression, but it was no longer running his life. Pet therapy not only helped Matty but indirectly saved Brody, too.

Discuss pet therapy with your therapist if it is a good option. They will have insight and recommendations.

FLOTATION THERAPY

Also known as sensory deprivation, flotation therapy requires that you immerse yourself in a tank of water and Epsom salt. The water is body temperature, the Epsom salt creates the buoyancy needed to give you a sense of zero gravity, and the tank (or pod) is soundproof. This shuts out all distractions for total relaxation. A bonus to Epsom salt is that it's most famous for its ability to relax your muscles, so a flotation therapy session soothes your mind and body simultaneously.

Flotation therapy can be especially great for those suffering from depression. It lowers your blood pressure and cortisol, taking you out of the consistently stressed state that depression leaves you in. Inside the tank, all the worries you brought can melt away, leaving only room for yourself. This is a beautiful time to practice slowing down your mind. You permit yourself to let go for only one hour per session. The deep relaxation induced by a session can last a full day, giving you much more relief from your hectic life.

If you've decided that flotation therapy may be for you, you'll want to ensure it's a viable choice in your area. Once you've scheduled your appointment, you can do a few things before your session.

Don't make the appointment in the middle of a busy day. The object is to promote serenity, so a flotation therapy session would be best on a day off.

Go easy on the big breakfast and coffee. The caffeine and a full stomach can be counterproductive. You may end up jittery and uncomfortable instead of fully relaxed.

Sensory deprivation tanks have an excessive amount of Epsom salt in them, so make sure you don't have any open wounds and don't shave.

Cleanliness is paramount since the warm salt water can breed bacteria. Even if a shower is provided in the facility, you should shower before leaving your house. Since you will be clean, bring any toiletries you need once the session ends.

Along with toiletries, you should bring something to record your thoughts and feelings once the session is over. You may even have an epiphany or two.

Flotation therapy can be the best supplement to your mental health care plan since its sole purpose is to block out everything except your heartbeat and breath. Your mind and body come together in harmony for total serenity.

NUTRITIONAL PSYCHIATRY

Nutritional psychiatry implements diet plans to encourage mental wellness. It uses the direct connection between the food you eat and how it affects your neurotransmitters.

Did you know 95 percent of your serotonin is produced in the gastrointestinal tract (Selhub, 2022)? Yes, that brain chemical that gives you good feelings. That means that whatever you feed it will have an impact. Nutrition isn't just for your physical health; it's for your mind, too. A diet high in processed food can't give you the essential vitamins, minerals, and proteins you need for a balanced mind and body. In today's instant gratification society, convenience usually wins over careful meal planning. Why prepare your meals the night before or get up early to cook when you have to hit the ground running every morning and pour yourself into bed late every night? Who has time for that nowadays? If you make the time, I promise you won't regret it.

Avoid processed food like the plague. That means regular sugar and artificial sweeteners. Vegan foods and lean protein are the best choices for mental and physical health. You can replace your chips with a homemade trail mix of almonds and dried fruit. Replace your burger with ground turkey and a whole-grain bun. Incorporating small changes into your diet will make the change go more smoothly.

When you have a checkup, ask your doctor about any vitamin deficiencies. If you do, make a point of adding a food rich in that vitamin to your diet. Supplements or medical intervention could be needed if your body has trouble absorbing nutrients.

All you have to do is make the conscious decision to choose health over convenience, and you'll be more naturally happy. You will be more focused and attentive, have more energy, and maintain your focus throughout the day. Sugary and processed food feed your depression, not you. It destroys the good bacteria in your digestive tract that produces serotonin. You'll be more tired, moody, spacey, and slow to react.

What Should You Eat?

Foods that are high in antioxidants (vitamin C, beta carotene, and E) will slow cell deterioration by reducing the free radicals your body produces. This deterioration can contribute to depression and other mental health issues.

Complex carbohydrates (brown rice, whole grains) are more beneficial for depression than simple carbohydrates (sugar, bread). There's a possible link between serotonin and carbohydrates, so choose the complex over the simple for a healthier mind.

Eating lean protein is essential for an all-around healthy lifestyle. It keeps all your muscles strong, including your brain. A good amount of protein in your diet will keep you focused and perceptive.

The Mediterranean diet is an excellent source of B vitamins and flavorful foods. If you decide to try it, you won't be disappointed.

Things high in selenium and omega-3 fatty acids, like fish, can reduce stress and boost mood.

Try to include foods like milk, turkey, Brazil nuts, carrots, clams, mussels, coffee, leafy greens, and salmon in your diet to reap their antidepressant qualities.

DIGITAL DETOX AND NATURE THERAPY

The digital age we live in today is mind-bending. We have information at our fingertips whenever we need it. We are more globally connected than ever before. We can talk to or text whoever we need anywhere. We have cars that park themselves. The advancements we have made in the last few decades are impressive.

Of course, there is another side to these marvels. Information overload, misinformation, and judgmental strangers criticizing your thoughts are just a few. How much is too much?

Too much screen time can lead to depression in several ways. You can feel bullied or invisible on social media. The desire to fit in is human nature, so being jilted—even by strangers on the internet—can hurt. On the other hand, if you have a following in your social circles, you may fear missing out or losing followers if you don't post for a day. In a way, our electronics are like drugs. The more time you spend with them, the worse you feel, but you can't seem to stop. Detoxing from the digital world is necessary to keep your mental health balanced.

Reducing Your Screen Time

I know it can be challenging to live without your phone, tablet, or computer 24/7, so here are some tips to get you started.

Record and keep a close eye on how much time you spend online. Some apps do this for you, which can help force you to keep to your restrictions. You can go old school and keep a memo pad handy. Keeping a record will cement it into your mind, and you'll see that you're picking up your device less often.

How many devices do you have, including televisions? Do screens surround you? If so, removing most of them will help you detox from technology.

You have to have a phone. It's a lifeline for almost everyone now and crucial for emergencies. You don't need the latest smartphone that costs as much as the down payment on a new car. If you're more invested in what's happening in that little rectangle than in front of you, it's probably time for a downgrade. Consider trading in the fancy gadget for one of those cheap prepaid flip phones. It will make the temptation to waste the day scrolling disappear.

Make time for tech-free breaks. Schedule them like an appointment and set an alarm. Soon, it will become a habit that you look forward to.

Find something that can be done with technology, but make a point of doing it the old-fashioned way. Read a book—or journal by hand. Visit a friend. Go for a walk without your fitness watch.

Establish firm rules and stick to them. That's harder than it sounds. As the day passes, you'll forget to pick up your device and absently pick it up. The more you practice, the easier it will become.

Turn everything off before bed. If you depend on your phone's alarm, turn off all notifications except that. The best thing to do is to have a separate alarm and turn the phone off so you're not tempted to check it if you wake up at night.

Physical complaints arise when you have too much screen time. Besides headaches and eyestrain, you could develop arthritis or carpal tunnel syndrome from too much scrolling and typing. When you take your breaks, a hand massage could help. Give your spine a break by alternating between sitting and standing, primarily if you work in front of a computer all day or are an avid gamer. Ensure your posture is as good as possible to reduce strain on your back and neck.

Natural Support

Spending time in nature can significantly enhance your depression treatment. The exercise alone will increase your endorphins, creating a sense of exhilaration that will last a while. Making it a habit will encourage your mind to choose serenity over despair.

Humans are animals. Our intelligence sets us apart from others, but we are still mammals. As much as we think we're above nature, Earth is our home. Our bodies are created to adapt to the environment, and it gives us what we need for healing. If you try to return to nature occasionally, you'll see that most of your stress melts away as you breathe in the fresh air. The extra oxygen intake will reinvigorate your entire system, including your brain. Spending a little time outside daily will improve your immune system, clear your head, and boost your imagination.

Getting outside to do nothing but experience nature can be difficult. You spend most of your days at work; then you have to go home, clean, cook, take care of kids, etc. We're undoubtedly busy for a society that is constantly in front of a screen. There are small ways to incorporate nature therapy into your daily life.

Get yourself some houseplants. They don't have to be any kind that requires too much attention; they are just something you can water once a week. Bringing a little nature into your home increases the oxygen and sunlight in the house. Sunlight is preferable to bulbs during the day. If stuck inside, you can listen to the nature-inspired ambiance on your favorite radio app.

A few minutes a day spent in nature can lower cortisol and relieve depression symptoms. Anyone going through a rough patch should consider starting an outdoor routine of quiet contemplation. You'll find the chaos in your head tempered, and your energy levels improve.

YOGA NIDRA

The word Yoga can make you think of painful stretches and impossible poses. With yoga nidra, all you do is lie down and allow yourself to be gently nudged into a deep trance. Yoga Nidra differs from other guided meditations because of its method and results. With other guided meditation practices, you are led into theta brain wave activity, the realm of dreaming. You remain awake, though, experiencing the euphoria of the words guiding you down. Yoga Nidra leads you to the delta brain wave state, the realm of the deeper subconscious. Here is where you can access your autonomous bodily functions—blood pressure, heart rate, and nervous system all fall into this category. Most meditations will have you seated comfortably to avoid falling asleep, but yoga nidra will have you lying down. You'll be in a deep sleep state while remaining conscious, so you will most likely lose feeling in your physical body.

What Can Yoga Nidra Do for You?

This time-honored practice can help you gain control over functions that are otherwise out of reach. With regular sessions, you will see an improvement in your immune health, stress, digestion, and memory. It can help regulate your sleep patterns, which are probably chaos if you're in the middle of a depressive episode. Your eating habits degenerate when you're depressed. You crave unhealthy foods or stop eating altogether. Yoga Nidra can help regulate your digestive system, improving your serotonin production. Yoga Nidra can also diminish headaches and other pain conditions. It encourages healthier thought patterns, minimizing depression and anxiety (Vallie, 2022). Starting a regular yoga nidra practice can only enhance your depression treatment plan, so don't be afraid to give it a go.

Getting Started

Yoga Nidra is a structured practice, so I've laid out the steps you need to take to get started (One Yoga, 2023):

1. Preparation
2. Initial relaxation
3. Sankalpa
4. Rotation of consciousness
5. Awareness of breath
6. Feelings and sensations

7. Visualization
8. Sankalpa
9. Externalization

To prepare for your yoga nidra session, lie on your back with your feet and arms slightly widened and your palms up. This is known as the corpse pose in Yoga. It's okay to get cozy. Use a pillow, blanket, and eye mask if that's what you need.

Focus on each body part from toes up one at a time. Feel each of them relax as you move your awareness upward. A promising sign that you're entirely relaxed is that you can no longer feel your extremities or your back pressing into the mattress. It's that weightlessness you feel right before drifting off to sleep.

Sankalpa means resolve or resolution. In this practice, you set your intention in a short statement and repeat it three times. You will use the same one every session until you meet your goal.

Keep sending your awareness to each body part, cycling back down and up again. You may fall asleep at this stage the first few times you try. That's okay; keep trying until you can stay awake.

Breathe normally, but pay attention as your stomach rises and falls. Try to count your breath 27 times. This is also a step where you may fall asleep. Keep at it until you succeed.

Physical and emotional feelings will come to the surface at this stage. Acknowledge and release them. If necessary, counter them with the opposite feelings. This will bring balance and refocus you.

You will visualize an image that brings you tranquility. If you're using a guide, they will provide the image. If you decide to try it independently, use what appeals to you. It's called visualization, but using all your senses in this exercise is essential.

Now is the time to reaffirm your resolve three times.

Take your time coming back to full consciousness. Rushing the process will shock your system and possibly undo everything you accomplished. First, notice your body and breath. Then, become aware of your surroundings. Last, slowly start to move your body and open your eyes.

Although it may be difficult at first to quiet your mind enough for this type of deep trance, the practice is worth it for its ability to bring you peace and comfort.

PAUSE AND PONDER

Therapy Exploration

Which novel therapy approaches in this chapter appeal to you most and why?

Integrating Approaches

Reflect on how you can integrate one of the novel methods discussed with any current treatments or therapies you are using. How might they complement each other?

SEGUE

Whether traditional or not, your treatment plan is crucial for your well-being and survival. For them to work correctly, you must understand yourself and your unique experience with depression. The next step of your J.O.U.R.N.E.Y. will teach you to understand your demons.

U - UNDERSTAND YOUR DEMONS

" *"Being able to be your true self is one of the strongest components of mental health."*

— DR LAUREN FOGEL MERSY

WHAT DO YOU KNOW?

J ust like being aware of your surroundings is more than just looking out the window to see if it's sunny, self-awareness is more than deciding what you want for lunch. It's the ability to recognize your innermost being for what it is. You know why you hold the ideals you do, make your own decisions, and what you get from the routines you've developed over the years.

It sounds simple enough, but most people must take the time to self-reflect. They're busy going through the motions of the mundane: They get up, go to work, do their job all day, and come home exhausted but still have household chores. The dog needs to be walked, the kids need help with homework, and they forgot to take something down for dinner. They're too tired to think. They get up the following day and do it all over again. They don't know why they feel the things they do or realize that they spend most of their time reacting on impulse.

When you're depressed, a practice of self-reflection will make you more aware of why and how you are the way you are. The more you understand, the better equipped you are to choose therapies that suit your needs.

WHY SELF-AWARENESS IS ESSENTIAL IN UNDERSTANDING DEPRESSION

Sometimes, depression does hit for reasons out of your Control, but most episodes have either an internal or external trigger. Once you understand those triggers and your reactions to them, you can do your best to avoid them. If unavoidable, you can intervene by doing what works for you to elevate your mood.

How to Develop Self-Awareness

Understanding that you're not as aware as you should be is a significant first step. Now, you're ready to take Control of yourself and your depression.

Keep a journal to record your thoughts and feelings as you experience them. This may seem like tired advice, but it works. Unless you're on a digital detox, you may have a phone with a notes app. If you want to text less, there's usually a voice recording app, too. Tracking your emotions, what may have triggered them, and even the weather conditions will give you a roadmap of your feelings and potential triggers.

This may set your teeth on edge, but getting input from those who know you best can be enlightening. Depression can come with a bit of paranoia. You become afraid that others are judging you as much as you judge yourself. This is false; your friends, family, and coworkers can give you honest accounts from a different perspective.

Without judging yourself, ask hard questions. Why do you hold the political views you do? What (if any) is your religion, and why do you believe in it? What is the best way to raise children, and why? Ask yourself these questions about anything that you firmly believe is a value. Now, ask yourself if your actions reflect that. If you still need to, you have a place to start making your actions align with your true self.

Believe it or not, reading stories will help you develop sympathy and understanding for others. Fiction transports you to another place, in the perspective of another person. It walks you through the lives of its characters, showing you all their thoughts, feelings, triumphs, and flaws. You'll find characters you love, characters you hate, and characters you love to hate. Ask yourself what it is about them that evokes these feelings.

When you're feeling pressured and down, take out your journal (or phone) and list a few things that make you feel grateful. A regular practice of this will lift your spirits. Getting into the habit of doing it daily will change your mindset from one of little to one of plenty.

Keep a close eye on your automatic reactions. Why did something make you angry or hurt? Are those feelings justified? Was it intentional on the other person's part, or did you take something wrong? Before you react, take a deep breath and allow yourself to calm down. After your mind has cleared, you can decide if you should be upset.

Take a few quiet moments each day to delve into your feelings. Accept them, even the bad ones, instead of trying to bury them. Ask yourself why you feel the way you do. If it's something you can change, take steps to do that. If it's something that you have no control over, let it go and shift your focus to something that makes you happy.

A Little Reminder

There is a difference between self-awareness and narcissism. Self-awareness is about knowledge. You can be brutally honest with yourself and who you are deep down. From there, you can determine what's good for you and what isn't, which techniques work and which don't. It alerts you to red flags from others and yourself. As you gain experience practicing intentional self-awareness, you'll see that every time you think, "Something told me I shouldn't have listened to..." that's not intuition. Your subconscious saw the red flags and tried to alert you, but you ignored them.

Narcissism is about gratification. It's the part of you that looks for others to agree, whether right or wrong. It tells you to numb your feelings instead of facing them because it would be too hard. Narcissism feeds into the lies that depression tells like a co-conspirator in a spy movie.

It's not what you want but what is best for you that makes you self-aware.

TOOLS FOR SELF-ASSESSMENT

Do you think you might be depressed but don't know where to start? These checklists will help you evaluate yourself. They are not a form of diagnosis, but they will help you determine if you need one. You will answer these questions with no, sometimes, or yes. Think of them as green, yellow, and red (regarding traffic lights). You're good to go if most of your answers are no. If most of them are sometimes, that's normal, but you should be more alert to problem areas. If most of them are yes, you should talk to your mental health provider.

- Are you experiencing moments of unhappiness more than moments of contentment?
- Are you losing interest in hobbies or activities that used to bring you joy?
- Do you binge eat or not want to eat at all?
- Are you tired all the time?
- Are you unable to get a full night's sleep?
- Are you sleeping too much?
- Do you feel like everyone is judging you?
- Do you feel like nothing you say or do matters?
- Do you have trouble focusing or remembering details?
- Do you think it would be better if you were no longer around?
- •Do you feel that if you hurt yourself on the outside, the pain on the inside will go away?

The last two are crucial. Even if the answer is sometimes, seek emergency care immediately!

RECOGNIZING TRIGGERS

A trigger is not something that directly causes your depression but something that brings it to the surface. For example, if you were in an accident and lost a parent when you were ten and struggled with depression, the song that was on the radio at the time could be a trigger. Here, we'll discuss possible triggers and how to manage them. Your triggers are as distinctive as your diagnosis, but I hope to give you an excellent place to start.

Identify Your Triggers

If you've lost someone in your life, anything that reminds you of them could trigger depression. You should also be aware of anything that could remind you of the circumstances of their death. Sometimes, these are subtle:

- A whiff of the type of flowers at their funeral.
- Hearing a word or phrase, they said regularly.
- Someone passing you on the street with the same eye color.

The moment was a split second, but your subconscious remembers everything.

If you lost your job, your significant other broke up with you, or you've been scorned in some other way, this could be a trigger. If you take events like this to heart, you could sink into a baseless cycle of unworthiness—especially if it's happened before. You will expect the circumstances to be identical to the last time, and the depression from the past could flare back up.

You're arguing with your spouse, the bills are due, and your paycheck is late, plus your doctor wants you to go on a low-cholesterol diet. Everyone has their stress and must find their ways to deal with it. If you don't have an outlet, the buildup could lead to a depressive episode.

Any type of sickness, chronic or acute, could be a trigger. It takes you away from your routines, and now you must focus on health-care. Your mind is constantly on the illness instead of your wellness. It's important to schedule yourself some time each day for an activity that makes you happy.

Life is busy. It's tempting to forego two hours of sleep here and four hours there to squeeze a little more out of the day. Exhaustion has its consequences in the long run. Among other problems, it breaks down your mental barrier and can trigger depression.

Do you tend to chew on a problem in your head? Do you obsess over it until it pushes out all other thoughts? Those thought obsessions could lead to depression. Be careful with your negative thoughts and emotions. Learn to let go. If it's something that you know you can solve, distract yourself for a while. The solution will come to you. There's no reason to dwell if you have no control over it. Dwelling is the trigger. It's more complicated than it sounds, but I'm here to teach you how to do it.

Money's tight for most of us. If that's not a problem, skip to the next paragraph. For those still reading, money is a significant source of stress. Worrying over the bills, doctor visits, supplies for the kids' school projects, and car maintenance is probably on your mind all day. You feel guilt when you can't afford something for your family. Each paycheck is a godsend; if anything happens to you, those who depend on you suffer. All this worry over money triggers depression in many people.

You graduated, got a great job, and negotiated your first mortgage —all great things, right? Except now you're homesick. You've gone from carefree to endless responsibility. Each milestone in your life is a necessary change for evolution, but even the incredible life changes have their downsides. Resistance to change can trigger depression in a big way. Even though you'll miss the way things were, you should always look forward to the amazing things to come.

Addiction is a complex subject to broach. Most who have a problem with addiction started it to mask emotional pain. When they realized that the drugs or alcohol only made it worse, it was too late. Not only is addiction a trigger for depression, but it can cause it. Alcohol and certain drugs are depressants themselves. Stimulant drugs upset your natural nervous system, making it hard to focus. When they wear off, the aftereffects cause depressive mood swings and lethargy.

Managing Triggers in Daily Life

Now that you have an idea of what could trigger your depression, how do you avoid it? Once you know your triggers, you can steer clear of a good number of them. Some are unavoidable, though, or take you by surprise. The only thing you can do when this happens is damage control.

One by one, you must determine your triggers. Take note of your initial reaction and the resulting depression. Were there exceptional circumstances, or was it something you encounter daily? Can you circumvent it next time? Details like these will increase your self-awareness and lessen your episodes.

Analyze that initial reaction. Was it helpful? A triggered reaction is usually one of anger or despair. Mindful of those reactions, you can learn to acknowledge and release your feelings. You'll know what's effective and what's not.

How could you have handled your most recent trigger differently? Visualize a scenario that offers you the best outcome for the situation. Can you apply it next time? This exercise will activate your problem-solving skills at a time when your instinct is to act on pure emotion.

Is there someone in your life who lifts your spirits? Your spouse, sibling, or even a pet? Maybe you find the most comfort sitting on a park bench, chatting with the elderly lady who goes there every day to eat her sandwich. Finding at least one person who can talk you down when triggered can be the difference between a full-blown episode and moving on.

The best scenario visualizations can be used here. Use them to map out a system of management and write it down. It must be handy when you're not thinking as clearly as you should. Don't overcomplicate it. Your frazzled mind can only process it if it's as easy as possible. What's important is that you can reference it when you need it.

THE POWER OF JOURNALING

There are so many advantages to keeping a journal, but it's hard to understand why everyone doesn't do it. Sometimes, sorting out your thoughts and emotions is hard, especially in a crisis. Taking the time to write them down will help you better organize and understand them. It engages your logical mind to override the emotional chaos, enabling you to deal with the crisis and move on. Over time, you'll develop the skill set you need to manage each setback as it happens.

As you gain those new skills, you'll see that you're not as distressed by your triggers as you used to be. You've moved out of that constant fight-or-flight mode and can quickly release your tension. It will make you more reflective than retrospective because you can see your emotions in a tangible form instead of dwelling over what should have been.

When you're in the throes of depression, it's twice as hard to focus. You feel the anxiety and hopelessness but can't say why, much less come up with solutions. Journaling will help you brainstorm those solutions, providing a way to direct your emotional energy better. Without an outlet, even a quiet one such as journaling, all those unspent emotions mash together and boil up like a bitter soup until there are no words or reasons to describe the anguish inside.

When you keep a journal, make it detailed. Record the date, weather, and anything else you feel is essential. Include that if you can pinpoint what happened before an incident or trigger. These details will help you recognize patterns you might otherwise miss, which are crucial to managing your trigger responses.

Recordkeeping is vital to cultivating self-awareness. It's only sometimes comfortable. It forces you to acknowledge thoughts, feelings, and memories you would rather keep buried. Now, you must face them so you can release them. A bucket can only be filled so much before it spills over, and that's the only thing that burying your feelings accomplishes.

As you stick with a daily journal habit, you'll become more assertive in the long run and better able to deal with your inner turmoil (Wright, 2023).

How to Start a Mental Health Journal

First, choose your medium. Would you be more comfortable with a notebook? Should it be a plain one or something a little fancier? If typing is more your style, your favorite word-processing program will do the trick. If you prefer to be more mobile and tech-friendly, there are plenty of apps for your phone. What's important is that it's easy and convenient for you to write daily.

Journaling can be easy to forget or procrastinate before it becomes a habit. It is a good idea to have something portable (a small notepad or your phone) to write your thoughts down as they come. You can set aside some time at the end of the day to organize them into your preferred journaling medium.

No one has to read your journal unless it's an assignment from your therapist to go over it during the session. Some people get anxious over the little details (Did I spell that word right? Does that sentence make sense?). Don't fret; get those thoughts down. I guarantee that your therapist doesn't care.

Don't be afraid to journal with a bit of flair. Art journaling exists, and incorporating visually appealing elements into your journal can help you express things you can't put into words.

When you're writing, avoid negative self-talk. This is a space where you can acknowledge your emotions without punishment. This practice is meant to relieve your mental load, not add to it. Write anything on your mind; if you don't know what to say, let your hands talk. By this, I mean let your mind go blank and start writing. You'll be surprised at what comes to the surface with this method.

Every once in a while, sit down and read through your past entries. Note any patterns you missed before and any changes you should have noticed. Looking back will tell you how you've grown in your journey and how much better your mental health has become. You'll see the shift from default negativity to positive thought patterns and habits.

Since this is a journal for your mental health, you must keep track of your symptoms. When a crisis hits, you and your therapist will know when it started and where to go.

Your journal will also help you sort out big, tough decisions. You can make out a list of pros and cons and sort out your feelings about each. This will help you to make less impulsive decisions, which could lead to regret.

Journal Prompts to Get You Started

Think about your ideal location, a space that would bring you peace and joy. Describe it and imagine yourself there. Is there anything you can do in life to work toward it?

Sometimes, you have so much chaos in your mind that finding a starting point is hard. Try these prompts to get the ball rolling:

- List things that made you feel good throughout the day. Be grateful for the small joys in your life.
- Every success today is worth noting, even if it seems insignificant. It helps you learn to give yourself due credit.
- Write everything you did during the day to lift your spirits.
- List anything you did to pamper yourself today. If you didn't get around to it, why not?
- Write out your plans for the day. Include anything extra you would like to accomplish. Pat yourself on the back when you achieve the extras.
- Find three more things you can do to pamper yourself and add them to your routine.
- Ask yourself what has sparked moments of joy today. Can you do it more often?
- Think about who you are versus who you would like to be. What can you do today to get closer to becoming that person?
- Be your own cheerleader. Write yourself a note. Fill it with compliments and encouragement.

- List at least five things you can do that bring you pure, ecstatic joy.
- Keep a monthly joy log. List everything that made you happy, and you'll watch it grow every month.
- Ask yourself if you encountered any triggers today. How did you handle them?
- Ask yourself what you need to cleanse from your life to be happier.
- With all your external responsibilities, write down things you can do to be more responsible for your inner being.

These are to get you started. Once you develop a routine, you'll come up with your own for a much more personalized and rewarding experience. Journaling is the most effective do-it-yourself therapeutic practice you can try.

EXERCISES IN SELF-REFLECTION

Use these self-reflection exercises to understand yourself better, your mental health, and your J.O.U.R.N.E.Y.

1. Ask questions that encourage more profound answers. Simple yes or no questions will not do when it comes to self-reflection. For example, ask, "How am I feeling? Why am I feeling this way? What can I do to change my mood?"
2. Don't delay in starting your journal. It's the most essential tool you have.
3. Find a meditation practice that suits you and stick with it. It doesn't have to be complicated or time-consuming. You will notice a positive difference with only a few minutes a day.
4. Anytime a major event happens (good or bad), take the

time to let it sink in. Use your journal to sort out your feelings about it (Gupta, 2023).

PAUSE AND PONDER

Think about everything you learned about yourself and your depression in this chapter. Did anything resonate with you? If not, here are a few suggestions to get you started.

Journal Prompt

Reflect on a recent day when your mood was low. Write about what happened, how you felt, and what may have triggered those feelings.

Trigger Tracking

Create a list of potential triggers you've identified and brainstorm how to manage or avoid them.

Self-Assessment Reflection

After completing the self-assessment tools, write about any new insights you gained about your depression.

SEGUE

Now that you have the tools you need to understand your depression and its effects fully, it's time to take the next step in your J.O.U.R.N.E.Y.: Reclaim Control. Managing your symptoms is essential but only a part of the puzzle. You'll learn to cultivate a more positive attitude in your daily life.

R - RECLAIM CONTROL

> *"You don't have to control your thoughts. You just have to stop letting them control you."*

— *DAN MILLMAN*

This powerful reminder by Dan Millman sets the stage for our journey in this chapter. Managing depression requires more than understanding—it necessitates action. Here, we will explore practical, hands-on techniques derived from mindfulness, relaxation, and Cognitive Behavioral Therapy (C.B.T.). These tools are designed to cope with demanding days and transform them into a pathway for personal growth and emotional resilience.

MINDFULNESS AND RELAXATION TECHNIQUES

Mindfulness is the conscious practice of staying entirely in the moment instead of dwelling on the past or worrying about the future. There are several ways to work on mindfulness, like meditation and focusing on every sensation as you go about daily tasks.

This forces your mind to step out of the past and into the present, effectively ending negative thoughts lingering in the back of your head.

Benefits of Mindfulness

Mindfulness is a sharp tool to diminish your depression symptoms by controlling your emotional responses and reducing your anxiety and other forms of stress. Anxiety is a sense of dread about something in the future; stress happens when you dwell on the past. You get stressed out because you had an anxiety episode a few moments before, and now you're stuck in that confusing loop. Bringing your consciousness back to the present breaks the loop.

Your memory and critical thinking skills will improve because you focus on experiencing every detail of the present moment. This will be essential in combating the brain fog that comes with depression and significantly improve both your home and work lives.

Mindfulness can also help deepen the connections you have with those around you. When you are entirely engaged in a conversation instead of your mind worrying over something that happened hours ago, the other person can tell the difference. You'll find that all of your relationships grow stronger.

Simple Mindfulness Techniques

Here are a few methods to practice mindfulness that I have found helpful in my journey. They are easy to do and don't consume too much time:

- Most people spend a lot of time in their vehicles. When you're not going to and from work, you're shopping, chauffeuring your children, or any other things that keep you busy. This is the perfect time to practice mindfulness. Is the air conditioning on? What does it feel like as it blows on your skin? Do you hear the tires rolling on the asphalt or your kids fighting in the backseat? Take a deep breath and notice how the steering wheel feels in your hands. If you're stuck in traffic or frustrated by that guy who cut you off, focus on taking deep breaths, counting them so that it fills your consciousness. Your frustration will melt away with each new breath.

- Take the time to stop and think about your next decision, like getting up for a glass of water. You usually do this automatically, and stopping to think about it brings you back to the present moment. Do this with every action that you tend to do without thinking. When the time comes to make big decisions, you'll be less inclined to act on impulse.

- How you wake up sets the tone for the rest of the day. Starting mindful will circumvent some of your daily stressors before they get to you. When you first wake up, take a few deep breaths and ask yourself what you want to accomplish today. For example, "I will be calm and productive today." Take a few more breaths and prepare for a calm and productive day.

- Do you eat in front of the television or gossip with friends? Do you mindlessly shovel food into your mouth while scrolling through a news blog? For your next meal, take the time to savor it truly. Relax before taking your first bite. Chew slowly and keep breathing. Notice the flavors explode on your tongue. Please pay attention to your stomach and stop when it's complete.

- Your exercise routine is the perfect time for this practice. Instead of blasting music or going through the motions, let the repetitive movements lull you into a mindful meditation. Focus on each breath, stretch, and rep as a first-time experience. When your workout is over, you should be relaxed and alert, no matter how intense it is (Pal et al., 2018).

Relaxation Techniques

A big step in reclaiming control over your depression is being able to relax at will. This will help you defuse your triggers and think more clearly. It takes practice, even for the healthiest and most peaceful person. Don't let this discourage you; the benefits far outweigh the lost time. When you've turned them into a routine, the techniques you learn here will come to you automatically. The effort won't take forever.

Breathing Exercise

Also known as box breathing, you'll picture each breath drawing a square. This exercise can be done anywhere:

- Take a deep breath and count to four before stopping. Imagine a line drawn upward.
- Hold your breath and count to four. Imagine a connecting line drawn across.
- Breathe out and count to four. Imagine the following connecting line going downward.
- Hold your breath and count to four. Imagine the last line connecting on the bottom. Your square is complete.
- Repeat as necessary until you're relaxed.

Progressive Muscle Relaxation

Progressive muscle relaxation (PMR) makes your muscles work for you instead of against you. It sounds counterintuitive, but consciously flexing a muscle and then letting it go drains the tension from your body. This is inconspicuous enough to do in public when you're feeling stressed.

- Get comfortable and breathe slowly.
- Pick one muscle group to flex. It's usual to start with your toes and work up to your head.
- Flex as hard as you can and release after a few seconds.
- Take that few seconds to evaluate how it feels. If that part is still tense, do it again. When it's relaxed, move on to the next muscle group.
- Work your way up until you've gotten all that you wanted. You don't have to do your entire body, just the muscles that hold the most tension.

Guided Imagery

This exercise has you build a picture that brings you peace and joy. It will be personal to you: a place, event, or someone's smile. It could be a favorite memory or a fantasy land with unicorns and waterfalls. There are no limits.

- Sit comfortably and close your eyes.
- Picture a place that makes you feel rested and at total peace.
- Don't just watch it like a television; put yourself there. You can feel the breeze and smell your favorite food cooking.
- Stay as long as you like. This is your special place to use in times of distress.

Meditation

The previous exercise is excellent for relaxation in times of sudden stress. Developing a regular meditation practice will allow you to shed all of the stress you've built up throughout the day. There are many different types of meditation out there. I've found this one to be the easiest to begin with:

- Sit comfortably with your feet flat and hands in your lap.
- Close your eyes.
- Keep your breath even and comfortable.
- If you have difficulty disposing of your negative thoughts, count your breaths to bring your focus back to the present. It's okay to lose count if you don't fall back into negative thinking.
- Try to hold this for at least 10 minutes. You can work your way up to 20 or 30 with practice.
- To bring yourself out of the meditation, wiggle your toes and fingers and open your eyes.

Self-Hypnosis

Self-hypnosis goes a step further than meditation. Instead of only concentrating on your breath, you have a goal when you hypnotize yourself:

- Again, sit and breathe comfortably.
- Set your goal. Make it short, something like, "I am relaxed."
- Repeat your goal as long as necessary until you're fully relaxed. You can have multiple goals, but focus on one at a time. Make sure they don't contradict one another.
- Keep repeating until you feel like you're in a trance.
- Bring yourself out by wriggling your hands and feet and open your eyes.

I've chosen the most straightforward exercises I know to get you started. Feel free to add more advanced practices to your routine as you progress (Lovering, 2022).

COGNITIVE BEHAVIORAL THERAPY (C.B.T.) BASICS

A lot less complicated than it sounds, C.B.T. is an intense therapy system that aims to train your mind to change your negative mentality. It's designed to be fierce so you can see results in a short amount of time.

Think of it as reverse brainwashing. Depression brainwashes you into believing all sorts of lies about yourself. C.B.T. is used as an active weapon to counteract this effect. With depression, your emotions do all the thinking for you, making you believe the negative things and disbelieve all the positive ones. It takes away your ability to make rational decisions because you'll think that the worst-case scenario is the only outcome. C.B.T. pushes your mind back into reality, encouraging you to look at the problem with a balanced point of view. You'll learn to think for yourself again instead of letting depression dictate your thoughts.

For C.B.T., you would have to work closely with your therapist. They will help you tailor the therapy to your needs, and you must be willing to do the required work. They will help you set a goal to concentrate on and train you to help yourself afterward so you don't have to go through it again. You will learn to analyze your own maladjusted beliefs and take control of them.

There is a rigid structure and time limit to C.B.T. It's like a laser pointed at a single problem, regular therapy being a fog light shining over your whole being. It uses different methods that are suited to your individual needs. At first, your therapist will have you focus on the present, but that may change as you progress (Zayed, MD, 2023).

Be prepared for your therapist to become a stern teacher during C.B.T. They will give you homework. You will get frustrated as your mind fights the change. Don't be discouraged. It will only last a few weeks; the rewards outweigh everything else.

Fighting Cognitive Distortion

A cognitive distortion is that part of your depression that tells you things like, "You're worthless; why bother?" None of it is accurate, and it is challenging to keep it at bay when in crisis. There are methods you can use to fight that nagging voice in the back of your head.

Everyone is against you. You do everything wrong. That woman you passed on the street hates your outfit. Your friend thinks you're a terrible driver. These are some of the things that depression tricks you into feeling. You can't possibly know what someone else feels unless they voice it.

Do you tend to overreact, making a situation seem worse than it is? We all do that sometimes, but I'm discussing taking it to the extreme. If someone is a few minutes late, you automatically imagine the worst-case scenario. If you haven't heard from someone in a while and they call you out of the blue, you automatically assume they have bad news. That's a pattern of thinking that you will learn to change.

On the other side of overreaction, maybe you jump in with both feet when you're excited by something. You're all in when you've decided to do something, and it becomes an obsession. If you can't do it all and do it right, you won't do it. You quit if it doesn't turn out like you thought it would. Your mind is lacking balance, but you will learn to fix that.

Your mind fills with all the things you didn't do and those you did wrong. Maybe you could say this instead of that. You should have taken a left instead of a right, but now you're late. Instead of lamenting over what wasn't done in the past, focus on the present. What can you do now?

When you're experiencing cognitive distortion, you feel that anything negative that happens to those around you is your fault. That barista isn't mad at you; they're having a bad day. Your coworker isn't crying because of anything you said or did; they just got some terrible news. You are not responsible for the moods of others, so don't shoulder that burden.

Cognitive distortion is the biggest liar you will encounter. C.B.T. will teach you how to destroy lies and see the truth.

Do-It-Yourself C.B.T. Exercises

Although C.B.T. does begin with intense sessions alongside your therapist, there are exercises you can do at home to start the process of reversing those self-defeating beliefs.

Trade Defeatism for Expert Problem-Solving Skills

It's hard not to fall into a negative thought cycle when something terrible happens, especially if you're already depressed. When you realize that you're wallowing in self-pity, stop. Take a breath. Ask, "Okay, this happened. Now, what can I do about it?" Be as specific with your question as you need to be. After practicing this, it will become a habit whenever you feel defeated. Soon, that will be your first thought instead of defeat.

Some things are beyond your control, and the answer to your question is "Nothing." Don't let that drag you down. If you can, let it go. If you can't, it's time to practice the relaxation exercises we discussed earlier. Whatever the crisis is, it will pass.

Revamp Your Perceptions

The way you see things determines the direction of your thoughts. When you get stuck in a cycle of negative feedback, sit down with your journal. Take a deep breath and think about the problem. Write it out and your thoughts about it. Write out good things that could come from it or express gratitude that it's not the worst. If you can't think of anything good, momentarily step away from the problem and write out all the unrelated good things in your life. Affirm to yourself, "I am grateful for these good things in my life, and this will pass quickly."

COPING MECHANISMS – SORTING THE EFFECTIVE FROM THE INEFFECTIVE

Everyone develops their coping mechanisms in life. These mechanisms help them deal with everything that comes their way. However, those mechanisms could turn toxic if they're not self-aware or don't have help.

The toxic ways of coping are called maladaptive. These are the things you do that make you feel either good or numb in the moment but aren't good for you in the long run. Drinking, drugs, binge eating, and shopping are all examples of maladaptive coping. What you're doing is distracting yourself instead of handling the problem. Not only that, but they could lead to severe health and financial issues.

This book teaches you adaptive coping mechanisms, which are healthy solutions. My goal is to teach you how to manage your depression in a healthy way that's accessible to everyone at any time.

Hone Your Coping Skills

If you're coping in a toxic way, you can learn to reverse your thoughts and turn them into healthy coping skills.

First, you need to study up on coping skills. You can choose this book as your guide or discuss it with your therapist. Choose one that appeals to you and try it for two weeks. From there, you can pick another to try or add another. This experiment is all about finding what works for you alone.

Anytime you have the urge to use a toxic coping mechanism, stop and take a deep breath. Switch gears and use your chosen healthy one. It will become a habit before you know it, and you will no longer automatically go for the toxic habit.

Just like any habit, it takes time and effort to change. It won't happen overnight, so don't be discouraged if you fumble a few times. Just keep trying, and you will get it. If you have too much trouble, discuss it with your therapist, and they can help you (Tracy, 2023).

Developing healthy coping skills is a tough job. It takes a lot of work and probably more than one failed attempt. It would help if you didn't let it get you down. Understand that there is no such thing as an instant fix when it comes to your mental health. Dust yourself off and try again. I promise it's worth it.

Joey's Story

Joey had just started as a freshman in college. Everything looked bright: he moved from his parent's house to a dorm, had a great major and big plans, and had a scholarship that covered most of his expenses.

It wasn't long before the stress of school started to build up. High school was easy compared to this. He always had good grades, but now he was struggling in almost every class. He stayed up all night studying most of the week, spent his days in class trying to stay awake, and began slamming energy drinks like they were going out of style.

He knew he couldn't keep up that pace for long. If he tried, he would end up on the drugs that several other students offered him. He couldn't have that. No matter how bad it got, he would never take drugs. Living on energy drinks and fast food wouldn't do, either. He felt more of a failure with each passing week and considered dropping out more than once.

Recognizing his problem, Joey turned to his roommate, Kenneth. A psych major would surely know what to do. The man was in his last year and seemed to have it all together. Kenneth gave Joey a bit of a blank stare as he vented his frustration. Without a word, Kenneth took the energy drink out of Joey's hand, tossing it in the garbage.

He told Joey that he took on too much for his first year. Instead of scaling back his workload to a manageable level, he had taken on coping mechanisms that were bad for his physical and mental health. It was a short conversation, but Joey knew his roommate was right.

It broke his heart, but Joey dropped one class. He spent that time on the gym treadmill, trading the fast food for a subscription that delivered all the ingredients for healthy meals. When he got frustrated with school, he would cope by taking a break and doing something fun. That three-minute conversation with his roommate changed his perception, encouraged him to keep going, and boosted his confidence. As a senior, he found himself giving a freshman the same encouragement.

PAUSE AND PONDER

You've learned several ways to reclaim your power in a time when you feel helpless. Here are a few exercises to get you started.

Mindfulness Exercise

Ten minutes a day is all you need to start a mindfulness practice. Use the methods you learned here and note how you feel afterward.

C.B.T. Challenge

Choose one negative thought you have often. Use the C.B.T. methods from this chapter to change it to a positive or neutral thought.

Toolkit Creation

Write down five strategies that appeal to you and include them in your toolkit for tough days. Plan when and how you can use them.

SEGUE

Now that you've learned how to replace despair with optimism, you're ready for the next step of your J.O.U.R.N.E.Y.: Nurture hope and positivity. You will learn ways to foster a positive and resilient mindset.

You Can Make a Difference

"Maybe there's a way out of the cage where you live. Maybe one of these days you can let the light in. Show me how big your brave is."

— SARA BAREILLES, "BRAVE"

As you advance in your personal J.O.U.R.N.E.Y. through the pages of this book, I hope that you feel a little less alone, misunderstood, and judged. Throughout this book, I have shared powerful stories of connection, understanding, and discovery. My aim in doing so was to reveal that when it comes to depression, it often takes one chance meeting, one step into new territory, and one moment of understanding to be the catalyst for transformation and change.

The defining moment in your journey could be a profound conversation with someone who helped you feel understood, not judged… or the words of a therapist who provided you with food for thought instead of dogma and instruction. It could be something within you that sparks a wish to move on… perhaps the act of forgiveness (or self-forgiveness), a moment of radical acceptance, or a chance activity that transforms into your life's passion.

The spark that pulls you out of a state of depression is so personal… thus, I have discussed a myriad of therapies, both traditional and alternative, to show that there are many paths to greater happiness. If this book has inspired you to walk any one of these paths, then I hope I can ask you to share your thoughts and opinions about this book.

By leaving a review of this book on Amazon, you'll let other readers with depression know that they don't have to force themselves to fit into someone else's mold.

If you wish, share a bit about your own story and the techniques that worked best for you. Your words could be that defining moment, the one that inspires someone to fight for a better, more meaningful life.

Scan the QR code below

N - NURTURE HOPE AND POSITIVITY

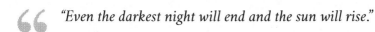

"Even the darkest night will end and the sun will rise."

— *VICTOR HUGO*

THE SCIENCE OF HAPPINESS

What exactly is happiness? It may seem like an abstract concept, distant and dreamy. It's not abstract at all. Happiness is a vital part of our nervous system and as crucial to our physical health as it is to our mental health. While past psychological efforts have revolved around the problem, positive psychology is a newer breakthrough in the field that focuses on bringing more happiness into your life (Sutton, 2020).

Happiness is dependent on hormone production. Imbalances or slower production can cause depression, low energy, and lack of clarity. Ideally, they all work as a team—each performing their tasks in harmony—to make sure you are as healthy and happy as possible:

Endorphins are the hormones that kick in when you do an intense exercise routine. They give you a brief rush of euphoria and relieve pain so you can push a little further. When you're in an emergency, the endorphins allow you to accomplish things you otherwise wouldn't be able to, like crash through a two-story window when the house is on fire. To naturally increase your endorphin production, start a rigorous exercise routine. If that's not possible, take the time to enjoy nature. Meditation and laughter are helpful, too (McCallum, 2021).

The serotonin neurotransmitter regulates mood, digestion, memory, and critical thinking skills. Exercise and natural sunlight are great serotonin boosters. Since most serotonin is produced in your gut, include probiotic-rich foods like yogurt.

Oxytocin is the hormone responsible for the instinct to find love and have a family. When you have chemistry with someone you just met, oxytocin is the chemical and the reason we connect with others. To increase oxytocin, get plenty of physical contact with your loved ones (pets count!). Hugs, cuddles, and other little shows of affection will boost your levels.

Dopamine is the neurotransmitter that triggers pleasure. When you take the first bite of your favorite meal or meet that deadline at the last minute, dopamine can also be triggered by things you're addicted to, such as alcohol or shopping, so make sure you choose healthy pleasures to increase your dopamine. Find something you like to do and make time for it. Practice compassion and get plenty of rest, or listen to music. All of these will give you a productive dopamine rush.

If you're anything like me, you prefer the abstract and dreamy over the hard-boiled science stuff. You'd instead feel your emotions and let them be, but it's vital to know the driving forces behind those emotions to understand and fight depression. So, take the time to learn about all those chemicals, what they do, and how to boost them. Your mental health will thank you.

FINDING JOY AMID THE GRAY

When you're in the middle of a depressive episode, it can feel like you're drowning. When you can open your eyes (awareness), everything is distorted. You can't see anything clearly, much less find a solution. Having a guide like this at your side is invaluable in times of crisis. Think of these tips, exercises, and inspirational stories as your construction crew. The foundation is your determination to become healthy again. Each time you use an idea from this book, you build another floor of happiness to protect you from the storms of depression.

Practical Tips

Humans are habitual by nature. Consciously plan a routine that promotes joy:

- Wake up with the affirmation, "I am happy today."
- Choose to look forward to work instead of dread it.
- Find several small ways to make yourself happy during the day.
- Before bed, write in your journal everything that made you happy and what you are grateful for today.

You are the person who takes the brunt of your foul moods. Here are some tips to show yourself a little love.

- When you impulsively insult yourself, stop and take a breath. Counteract the insult, saying, "No, you're brilliant."
- If you find yourself in an uncomfortable situation, don't be afraid to leave. Don't feel guilty; please don't worry about

what others will think of you. "No" is the most powerful word for your peace of mind.

- Meditate and do breathing exercises. Start with the meditation in this book, and work your way up to more intense practices.
- Nobody is perfect, so don't expect it from yourself. You will make mistakes and have setbacks. Forgive yourself and then work on a solution.

Depression loves to take our dreams and aspirations and grind them to dust. You can get them back if you work to redefine your sense of purpose.

- What has consistently been important to you? Could you write it down? It can be more than one thing. If it is, that's great. Recognize that this means that depression hasn't taken everything from you. At least one of these things can be a stepping stone to your purpose.
- Understand that having a purpose doesn't mean it has to be world-changing. It only has to improve your life.

Creativity expands your mind, calms your nerves, and soothes your soul. Here are some tips to incorporate creativity into your mental health plan.

- If you've never done anything creative, start with adult coloring books. Their intricate designs are more complicated than those geared toward children. Coloring is calming while adding a brilliant visual element to meditate on.
- Anything creative that appeals to you applies, whether writing, finger painting, crocheting, or macaroni sculpture.

It doesn't matter as long as you enjoy it and create something new.

- Remember, natural talent is not a requirement. You only have to enjoy yourself. Create without judgment. Since you are your worst critic, this is a great time to practice quelling that criticism.

If you have pets, spend more time with them. It's good for both of you.

- Pet cuddles release dopamine and oxytocin, making you feel euphoric and loved.
- It's nice to have someone always thrilled when you come home.
- Taking care of an animal is always appreciated, and it shifts some of your focus away from your negative thoughts.

Body movement is essential to hormone production. Here are some tips for mood-boosting exercise.

- Don't worry about your fitness level. If you have limited movement due to disability, that's okay, too. Do what you can, when you can. Every little bit counts.
- If you're you can, walk outside when possible. The fresh air and sunshine are preferable to a treadmill. Take it slow. The goal is to relax.
- Tai Chi combines meditation and movement and is excellent for cultivating joy.
- Slip in small ways to move more into your daily tasks, like parking at the end of the lot, dancing around while you clean the house, or circling the store a few extra times before checking out.

Therapy can be cleansing and rewarding, even if you're not having a crisis.

- Your therapist will listen to you without judgment and guide you in areas you feel stuck.
- Therapy is a safe space in an unsafe world.
- In therapy, you will learn skills to prevent a crisis before it can take hold of you.

Mood-Boosting Activities

Certain activities are well known to lift your spirits. These simple suggestions will get you started, and you can add to them as you discover things that work well for your needs.

- Binge eating is an unhealthy coping mechanism, but mealtime can also be a healing time. Plan and cook a healthy meal. Invite friends. Alternatively, you can invite friends out to a nice restaurant. There is no downside to good food and good company.
- Studying a new language is a great mood booster because it expands your mind, distracts you from your worries, and gives you the dopamine reward of learning something new. If you start stressing about something, you can practice your words, bringing your focus to the present.
- Read a book. Make sure it's an uplifting or exciting story. True crime and horror aren't appropriate for this exercise. A good story will place you in that world, so you want one that makes you feel good. You'll have the added benefit of walking in someone else's shoes for a while, making it a temporary, healthy escape.

- When depression hits, you may want to shut yourself away due to negative self-talk. Make room for family time. Have a barbecue or host a game night. Call or text a loved one every day. Ensure everyone you care about is aware that you think of them often.
- Think of something you've always wanted to do but couldn't. Skydiving would be an extreme example, but any challenge you find intriguing will do. Conquering challenges encourages growth, and the high of accomplishment will boost your mood for a long while.
- Texting is fast and convenient, but take time out of your day to call a friend. Hearing the voice of someone you love will alleviate your loneliness and help you feel like you're the important person that you are.
- Acts of kindness benefit the receiver, but the giver feels good having done something for someone else. If you cannot join a volunteer program, more minor acts of kindness throughout the day will surely lift your spirits.
- Keyboards have become routine, but typing doesn't convey the emotion that handwriting does. Try to handwrite something, like your journal, every day.
- While you're at it, sit down and write a letter. Not an email, but a handwritten letter that you will put a stamp on and mail. Writing itself is soothing and gives you a sense of satisfaction that pressing the send button doesn't. The recipient of the letter will appreciate it, too (Baylor Scott & White Health, 2020).

Not everything in life is one giant, joyful event. The little things build up to bring you joy if you take the time to savor them. Taking care of yourself means nurturing your happiness and, in turn, nurturing your soul.

THE POTENTIAL OF OPTIMISM

Optimism is the perception of hope instead of dread. An optimist in a fender bender will be grateful that no one was hurt and the damage wasn't bad. A pessimist will lament the repair cost and inconvenience and swear they have whiplash. Both were in the same accident, but their perceptions are different. Changing your perception will take some work, but it's well worth it for your peace of mind.

Would you rather be the one to say, "I have a good feeling about this," instead of, "Whatever can go wrong, will?" You've probably been conditioned to believe the latter, but there's a 50/50 chance either way. Optimism is the minor point of view, with pessimism being dominant. It doesn't make sense because it's a chosen point of view. Like all habits, it eventually becomes part of you without realizing it.

The key to healthy optimism is to be realistic about it. Naive optimism can do more harm than good. If you're ready to meet your challenges with a clear understanding of the risks involved, it's better to forge ahead with the hope that it will all work out. You can replace anxiety with anticipation, which is much more appealing to your mental health.

Strategies for Cultivating a More Positive Outlook

Even if you're a natural-born pessimist, you can retrain yourself to be more optimistic. It's as simple as flipping your perception in any given situation.

Pessimism is a way of worrying about the future. Use the techniques from this book to bring yourself back to the here and now. After a few minutes, please return to the issue with determination and look at it from a more hopeful point of view.

Pessimism can become a mountain of negative jabber in your head if not kept in check. It can add to or trigger depression. To counteract this, take a deep breath, close your eyes, and look inside your mind. Calmly respond to every negative thought with something positive. After you've calmed down, take out your journal and write only the positive counteracting thoughts.

When everything seems dire, and you can't stop dwelling on the problems, count five things you're grateful for. If you're still concerned, take a deep breath and count five more. Keep going until you're calm again. Gratitude is a building block of optimism. When you have something to be grateful for, you have something to look forward to.

Make an effort to be kind to others. This includes the people you know and strangers you interact with daily. You never know what kind of challenges they might be facing in their personal lives, and they don't see what you're going through either. You can make their day a little brighter by showing kindness and compassion towards everyone, including that grumpy cashier. Consistently practicing this habit of kindness can also help you become more optimistic.

Pessimism and skepticism go hand in hand. You may balk at consciously being more optimistic. Your mind, in the middle of depression, will try to convince you that any positive thought is silly and unrealistic. Ignore that and choose to think positively. Say it out loud. Write it in your journal. Make it a declaration of intention to break free from your depression.

Depression loves to blow things out of proportion. Its emotional and hormonal imbalances make you want to cry or lash out at the slightest inconvenience. You can defeat this reaction by doing the exercises you learned here. At the end of each exercise, pause and think of one good thing that happened today and one thing to look forward to tomorrow.

The way you speak reflects how you feel inside. Changing the words you use can have a massive impact on your mental health:

- Replace "I can't do anything right" with "I'll get it next time."
- Instead of "I'm worthless," try "I'm doing my best."
- "I'll never get it" can be "I'm working on it."

These aren't unrealistic, just more positive than the doomsday phrases.

Picture the outcome you want instead of the outcome you fear. Visualization isn't a fad or something touted by fake gurus. It's so popular because it works. It's a critical part of problem-solving and independent thinking. Imagination is the key to innovation, which you tap into when you visualize.

Affirmations are short statements of intent that start with "I am." Repeating these statements can help train your mind to achieve your desired state of being, such as calmness or positivity. Try to use the same one at the same time every day for at least a month. That gives your mind time to absorb it fully.

Changing your mindset to one of optimism can be a long process. In the meantime, adopt the mannerisms and speech of an optimist. Those around you will notice the difference, and it will help the process go faster.

TRIUMPH OVER ADVERSITY: INSPIRING STORIES

Gennifer

Gennifer was ecstatic. She had just made a new friend, Alissa. It turned out that they should have met 20 years ago, as they grew up not far from one another. Alissa only lived a few blocks away, but they met online. Gennifer invited her over for coffee, and they immediately hit it off. They shared so many interests, opinions, and ideas that they could have been sisters. They were both stay-at-home moms, so they were both thrilled to have an adult conversation.

Not even a month later, Gennifer checked her social media and saw a message that crashed her entire world. A relative of Alissa's posted that she'd had a stroke and passed away. Just like that, Gennifer's new best friend was gone. Of course, Gennifer had lost people before, but never so suddenly. She used to believe that everything happened for a reason, but now she questioned the senselessness of it all.

Depression hit hard and fast. She withdrew from her husband and kids, doing only the bare minimum in a blank haze. She ignored her friends and family, fearing another death. She gave up on all her interests and only focused on chores. Most of her time was spent in her bedroom. If she wasn't crying, she was sleeping.

After two months of despair, her wonderfully supportive husband stepped in. He asked her to get in the car, stopped for food, and took her to her favorite park for a picnic. They ate while she talked about Alissa and vented her feelings. In the end, she was sobbing in his arms while she let it out. When the sobs dried up, he asked her something that hadn't occurred to her, "Why aren't you meditating on it?"

Gennifer had been practicing regular meditation for decades. When the depression sank its teeth into her, she forgot about it. She could think of nothing else except Alissa and death. His support and words woke her up. She became determined to regain herself and become worthy of her husband and kids again.

It was a work in progress, but she started her meditation practice again and added a journal. At least once a week, she would return to that park alone to count her blessings. She was lucky to meet a beautiful soul like Alissa before she died. Her husband was terrific in helping her deal with it. Her kids were patient because Mommy was having a hard time. Despite the rough patches now and then, life was good.

David

David had always been a moody child. He would throw tantrums for no reason, crying for hours on end. He had headaches every other day and couldn't communicate what was wrong. At first, his parents didn't understand. They would punish him for his tantrums and make it worse. It was an everyday cycle, and no one in the house was happy. As he got older, the tantrums turned into violent outbursts. He would kick the wall with tears streaming down his face. He would throw things to vent his frustration. By the time he was 13, he had started banging his head into the walls and hurting his hands by punching anything hard he came across. His parents finally realized that something was seriously wrong and took him to a psychiatrist.

The psychiatrist diagnosed him with M.D.D. and prescribed medications to correct the chemical imbalance in his brain. He recommended a therapist he trusted for regular sessions. His parents apologized to him for not figuring it out sooner.

Now a happy adult, David looks back on his childhood with gratitude. He is thankful that the problem was found when it was. He had an answer and wasn't just a bad kid. His parents went to therapy with him, and they learned how to handle his episodes without punishment. Then, the family got closer. He wasn't cured. His treatment was ongoing, but he worked hard and lived a happy and productive life.

Tinlee

Tinlee was in her twenties and having the time of her life. She had many friends and a good job that paid for an apartment she rarely saw. She would go to work, come home long enough to shower and change and go clubbing with her friends. She would finally crawl into bed at two in the morning, wake up at eight, and do it all over again.

Everything changed when she got the flu. It was the worst she had ever been sick. She couldn't go to work or out with her friends. She was tired and feverish but couldn't sleep. All she could do was lie there and think.

Her friends never called to check on her, and she realized they weren't true friends. They were just people to party with. She had been living in the fast lane to distract herself from her profound loneliness. What she needed was a faithful companion. Once she got better, she went out and got herself a puppy.

Now, her clubbing money was spent on doggy daycare, and she had someone always happy to see her after work. Those "friends" never called, but she didn't care. She no longer dreaded going home because she had someone who loved her unconditionally.

"I used to think the worst thing in life was ending up alone. It's not. The worst thing in life is to end up with people that make you feel all alone."

— *ROBIN WILLIAMS*

MINDSET MATTERS: THE PSYCHOLOGICAL ANGLE

Changing your perception to one of optimism facilitates your recovery from depression. I'm not telling you to think happy thoughts and get over it. It doesn't work that way. By changing your perception, you can slowly push your depression out. It's you telling your subconscious that it's not welcome. Combined with your other treatments, you can overwhelm the depression like a wave washing over the sand.

Like negative thoughts feed depression, positive thoughts feed recovery. By intentionally focusing on the positive, serotonin increases and boosts mood, energy, and endorphins. A good cycle of mental health replaces the bad.

Cognitive Psychology

In the last chapter, you learned about C.B.T. and what it could do for you. How can you use it to maintain your optimism?

Because C.B.T. is so intense, you can restructure your thought patterns twice as fast. Your therapist will help you identify the lies your mind is telling you ("You're worthless!") and flip them around toward the truth. Depression will also make up baseless disaster scenarios that C.B.T. can target and destroy. It will lead you back to the more optimistic scenario where you have a problem that can be solved.

First, you must be self-aware enough to recognize a thought, emotion, or action that brings you down. It may take some practice, but I hope you've been doing the exercises from the previous chapters. If so, it will be much easier.

Challenge the thought you've recognized. Ask yourself if it's true. Can it be proven, or are you overreacting? Is it an assumption or based on an assumption? Are you going from point A to point C without considering the middle?

Now, picture the more favorable outcome. Feel the satisfaction of it. Say it out loud. Repeat this last part as often as needed until you no longer feel the negativity.

DAILY HABITS OF POSITIVITY

Building a routine of positive thinking will hammer it home, effectively retraining your mind to think the way you want it to.

- When you're in a cycle of self-deprecation, you tend to see everything you can't or do wrong. Flip that on its head by concentrating on everything you can do, everything you're good at, and everything you enjoy.
- Being thankful for your blessings is much better than bemoaning what you lack. Think of at least five things to be grateful for every day.
- Learn to forgive yourself. Mistakes happen. Acknowledge them and keep trying.
- Do one thing every day to pamper yourself. Whether it's a bubble bath and a good book or a moment of quiet contemplation before work, it must feel like a luxury to you.

- Interrupt your negative thought cycle with a healthy distraction. For example, spend time with your cat, call a friend, or solve a crossword puzzle.
- Intentionally look on the bright side. Nobody wants to wake up every morning to a screaming alarm, but choose to be grateful that you woke up. You've been criticized at work, and now you're seething. Take a deep breath, acknowledge your mistake, and vow to improve.
- A short meditation on love and kindness before you start the day is a great way to keep a positive frame of mind.
- Before you sleep each night, set positive goals for the following day. Having clear goals will slow down some of the chaos in your mind.

It generally takes two weeks for a practice to become a habit. Don't give up; soon, you will default to the optimistic frame of mind. Each exercise enriches your personal growth toward a more hopeful outlook.

PAUSE AND PONDER

It's time to reflect on this chapter and how you view optimism. Here are a few exercises for you to try before moving on.

Happiness in Action

Pick a time this week when you felt a moment of happiness. Where were you, and what were you doing? Can you incorporate more of that into your daily routine? If so, make a plan and do it.

Optimism Challenge

What are your challenges right now? Pick one and write it down in your journal. Brainstorm solutions, write positive thoughts about them, and log possible favorable outcomes.

Joy Journaling

Joy journaling, or gratitude journaling, is a transformative and uplifting practice that involves documenting things that bring joy, gratitude, or happiness. This activity is a powerful tool to shift our focus from the negativity that often engulfs us, especially during challenging times. Expanding on joy journaling, we can delve into its numerous benefits, effective methods, and practical tips for seamlessly integrating this habit into our daily lives.

Benefits of Joy Journaling

1. **Improved Mental Health**: Regular joy journaling can reduce stress and anxiety. By focusing on positive experiences, individuals can shift their mindset from scarcity or fear to abundance and peace.
2. **Enhanced Self-awareness**: Keeping a joy journal encourages you to observe and reflect on what truly makes you happy. This heightened awareness can lead to better decision-making and more intentional living.
3. **Strengthened Emotional Resilience**: Writing about joyful moments can help you relive them, which enhances positive emotions and reduces the impact of negative ones. Over time, this practice can help build resilience against depression and anxiety.
4. **Boosted Memory and Mood**: Recalling and recording happy memories can increase serotonin levels, a

neurotransmitter for enhancing mood. This can also help in forming lasting memories associated with positive feelings.

5. **Improved Physical Health**: Studies have shown that practices like joy journaling, which increase positivity and reduce stress, can lead to physical health benefits, such as lower blood pressure and improved immune function.

How to Practice Joy Journaling

1. Choose a Medium: Decide whether you prefer a physical journal, a digital app, or simply a document on your computer. The key is consistency and ease of access.

2. Set a Routine: Dedicate a specific time of day for journaling. Whether it's morning to set a positive tone for the day or evening to reflect on the day's joys, a routine helps solidify the habit.

3. Be Specific: Instead of writing broad statements, delve into what made you happy. For example, instead of noting "I enjoyed lunch," detail "I savored the crunchy, tangy salad at lunch with my best friend, laughing about old times."

4. Include the Small Things: Joy doesn't only come from significant events. It can be found in small, everyday moments, such as the warmth of a sunny window, the smell of coffee, or a smile from a stranger.

5. Reflect on Challenges: Sometimes, finding joy in challenges can be transformative. Reflect on what a harrowing experience taught you or how it might have led to unexpected positive outcomes.

6. Use Prompts: If you find yourself stuck, use prompts such as:

- What made me smile today?
- Who or what am I grateful for today?

- What's something I'm looking forward to tomorrow?
- What's a challenge I overcame today, and what did I learn from it?

7. Include Visuals: If you're artistic, or even if you're not, adding doodles, stickers, or pasting in photographs can make your joy journal more engaging and personal.

8. Review Regularly: Make a habit of looking back over your journal weekly or monthly. This can reinforce the positive feelings and help you see patterns of joy you may want to cultivate further.

Integrating Joy Journaling into Your Life

Integrating joy journaling into your daily routine is a powerful yet flexible tool that can be adjusted to fit any lifestyle or preference. Whether you dedicate several minutes or just a few seconds each day, consistently noting joyful moments can transform your outlook, making you more mindful and appreciative of life's blessings. This adaptability empowers you to make joy journaling a part of your life in a way that feels most comfortable and beneficial.

SEGUE

Like a beautiful houseplant, joy and optimism must be gently cared for. They will shrivel up and die if they're neglected, so take care of yourself, and yourself will take care of you. Now you're ready for the next step of your J.O.U.R.N.E.Y.: Embrace long-term healing.

E - EMBRACE LONG-TERM HEALING

> *"Once the storm is over, you won't remember how you made it through, how you managed to survive. You won't even be sure whether the storm is over. But one thing is certain. When you come out of the storm, you won't be the same person who walked in. That's what this storm's all about."*
>
> — *HARUKI MURAKAMI*

The road to recovery is a complex path. It is a journey that takes time, patience, and perseverance. No miracle drug or genie in a bottle can magically make you better. Recovery is a work in progress that must be handled with compassion and determination.

SUSTAINING PROGRESS WITH LONG-TERM STRATEGIES

Making a change can be difficult. For some reason, it seems easier to stagnate in depression than to take steps to claw your way out of it. Incorporating these things into your routine will expedite your success in seeking long-term mental health.

- Physical exertion is the best endorphin booster. You don't have to start a rigorous exercise program; move your body more. Take the stairs more than the elevator. Park a couple of blocks away and walk. Little changes add up to significant changes.
- Say no to junk food. It's fast, convenient, and full of, well, junk. Eat fresh food and drink plenty of water. Add yogurt and nuts to your diet to help your serotonin production.
- One of the critical symptoms of depression is insomnia. Try the relaxation exercises in the previous chapters to ensure you get your eight hours.
- When you're overwhelmed and frustrated, do something that soothes you. It could be art, crochet, coloring, or pounding on a bag. Anything that ends in relaxation will work.
- Remember to write in your gratitude journal. List everything you are thankful for at the end of the day, and you will be looking for things to be grateful for tomorrow.
- Anytime you have a negative thought, concentrate on the more constructive side of it. Can anything good come of it?
- Isolation and loneliness are depression feeders. Please don't give in to them. Stay in contact with your true friends and family. You need a support system now more than ever.

Mental Health Check-ins

Remember, you don't have to do everything yourself in this struggle. Your therapist is there to guide you through it. Checking in with them is vital to your recovery process. Your therapy sessions are a safe space to find the structured support you need to encourage healthy coping mechanisms and your evolution. If you consistently practice the techniques you learn here with the guidance of your therapist, you're sure to see a profound change in your way of thinking and way of life.

THE ROLE OF GRATITUDE

Touched on briefly in the previous chapter, now I'm going to take you for a deep dive Into the importance of nurturing gratitude for your mental well-being:

- Gratitude can help you reset when an ugly thought pops into your head. All you have to do is let the negative thought pass and follow it up with something you're thankful for. It doesn't have to relate to the evil thought as long as the feeling of gratitude is there.
- When consistently practicing, the above will become second nature and raise your overall perspective.
- Gratitude encourages you to aim higher. When you've accomplished a goal, be thankful for the ability to do so and set another.
- When you're thankful for the people in your life, you'll be more inclined to keep in touch. This will help you defeat the isolation of depression.
- A grateful attitude can shield you from most of the side effects of stress. Its calming effect counteracts the tension.

Gratitude: Make a Habit out of It

Forming a new habit requires consistency, so here are a few tips for long-term gratitude practices:

- Your gratitude journal is your best friend for building a habit. Make it portable so you can use it anytime you need a boost. At the very least, write everything you've been grateful for that day before bed.
- Intentionally cancel out your complaints with gratitude. For example, if your server trips and spills your lunch all over you, counter the initial anger with gratitude that the server wasn't hurt. Be thankful you weren't seriously burned. If you were, be thankful it didn't end with a trip to the hospital.
- When depression takes hold, it's expected to be angry at the world and take it out on those around you. A little bit of humility is in order here. Not so much as to fall back into negative self-talk but realize that it's not their fault. It's not your fault, either. Understand how lucky you are to have a support system and treat them kindly.
- Let those you are grateful for know that they are appreciated. It will make them feel good and will lift your spirits, too. They will be more inclined to keep supporting you.
- It's hard to look on the bright side when in a crisis, but it's vital to make a habit out of gratitude. When something negative happens, think about what good can come of it or what lesson you could learn.
- Volunteering is an excellent way to nurture gratitude. Whether it's time or money, giving to those less fortunate makes you think about all the blessings in your life.

According to Nathaniel Lambert, Frank Fincham, and Tyler Stillman, in a study conducted in 2012, gratitude has a positive effect on depressive symptoms. The study comprised eight trials, which showed that gratitude is linked to reducing depressive symptoms. Positive reframing and positive emotion were the two main mechanisms that accounted for this relationship. Studies 2-5 showed that positive reframing influenced the relationship between gratitude and depressive symptoms, while studies 6-7 demonstrated that positive emotion mediated this relationship. Study 8 found that positive reframing and positive emotion simultaneously influenced the relationship between gratitude and depressive symptoms. Overall, the study concludes that gratitude is an effec-tive tool in reducing depressive symptoms.

In another study, Nicola Petrocchi and Alessandro Couyoudjian write (2015):

The study found that gratitude is a significant predictor of reduced symptoms of depression and anxiety among the general population. The study also evaluated three types of self-relating processes as possible mediators of this relationship. These processes include trait gratitude, depression, anxiety, and three forms of self-relating, namely criticizing, attacking, and reassuring the self. The study involved 410 participants. The results showed that gratitude is associated with fewer depression and anxiety symptoms.

Moreover, the study found that the three forms of self-relating partially mediated the impact of gratitude on both depression and anxiety.

Interestingly, self-reassuring had a more substantial mediation power than self-attacking in the prediction of anxiety symptoms. The study concludes that gratitude is a protective factor against psychopathology due to its association with better relationships with others and a less critical, less punishing, and more compassionate relationship with oneself. (Pages 191-205)

RECOGNIZING WHEN TO SEEK PROFESSIONAL HELP

How do you know if your mental health is bad enough to start therapy? Everyone has mood swings, bad days, and upsetting events. The concept of mental maintenance can seem abstract and confusing.

Don't ignore your physical symptoms. Pay attention when your sleep patterns get weird, when your appetite changes, or when you start getting frequent headaches. Those are the first signs that something is off with your mental health (B. Johnson, 2020).

You'll notice your energy level take a nose dive. Not only do you become lethargic, but you've lost your will to do anything. Then you feel guilty about doing nothing. Romantic encounters are out of the question, and so are nights out with friends. We've discussed all this before, but when do you need outside help?

If your symptoms last over two weeks and tend to pile up on one another, it's time to make an appointment. If you're having thoughts of hurting yourself or others, it's time to get emergency services involved. Catching your symptoms as early as possible will prevent the worst.

Finding the Right Mental Health Professional

You've determined that you should get some help. When you're struggling with mental health, it can be overwhelming to know where to start. Knowing what's best for you isn't easy with many types of professionals and therapies available.

At this point, you need to find a mental health clinic near you. If the therapists there can't accept new patients, they may have a suggestion for you. After a therapist evaluates you, you can decide on the next steps together. You may see that therapist regularly, or they may recommend a psychologist or psychiatrist. It depends on your symptoms and what type of treatment you need. From there, you'll determine if talk therapy will suffice or if you need deeper treatments like medication and C.B.T. They may also recommend other treatments outside therapy sessions, such as support groups or yoga classes. Most importantly, you must be willing to do the necessary work to improve.

Don't Be Afraid to Ask for Help

Needing help for depression is not a weakness. Many people feel ashamed to ask for help when it should be the opposite. In admitting that you're not in a place to help yourself, you are committing an act of bravery. Be proud that you recognize your depression for what it is— an illness that needs medical care. Even if you're skeptical, be honest with yourself and your therapist. They will help you sort that out, too.

PREPARING FOR LIFE'S UPS AND DOWNS

Like it or not, life is about struggle. With each conflict, we evolve— individually and as a species. The trick is to adapt to our conflicts. Change is inevitable. You'll struggle, have setbacks, and eventually overcome it all. When you're prepared mentally, the changes will be for the better.

Those with depression tend to either blow everything out of proportion or choose to go into denial. Try to find that middle ground in the real world. Accept your challenges so you can face them. You can't wish your problems away, but with determination, you can find solutions to improve them.

There is no quick fix for depression. Those searching for one usually choose unhealthy dopamine rewards like junk food, shopping, or drugs and alcohol. These ultimately defeat your purpose. Recovery is a process that tolerates no shortcuts.

Remember to counter every negative emotion with gratitude. This cannot be stressed enough because of its direct impact on your depression.

Recovery from depression doesn't mean to banish all evil thoughts. It would help if you accepted them, or they'll hang around, waiting to be noticed. All your thoughts and emotions, even the bad ones, define who you are. The point is to change your perception so the good will come to outmatch the bad.

Life is filled with triumphs and failures. Embrace them all as learning experiences. Hard lessons can only grow you personally.

Build Resilience and Maintain Balance in Tough Times

When you're struggling, it's hard to see your way through to the solution on the other side. Here, I will give you the tools to include in your routines to keep you strong and balanced.

Meditation

Hopefully, you've already started a meditation routine. This will help you stay calm in the middle of the chaos. You can change the focus of your meditation to include strengthening your resolve. You can repeat affirmations throughout the day, such as, "I am strong. I am focused. I am balanced."

Forgiveness

Forgiveness isn't about absolving the other parties of their wrongs. It's about you and your peace of mind. This includes yourself. Show yourself the same kindness you show others and that you would like someone to show you. Forgiveness and self-love go a long way in building your resilience.

Flip the Script

Chewing on a problem makes it grow. Stop and reset if you're dwelling instead of trying to find a solution. Look for something positive to come from the situation:

- A lesson you could learn.
- Something to be grateful for buried in the problem.
- Something that you can do to pick yourself up (spa day, anyone?).

This changes your focus and brings you out of that negative time loop.

Conquer Your Fear

This one is tough. Fear is a biological response meant for survival. The majority of people today don't have that in mind. You go to work, make your money, and buy your food. The instinct of fear still exists, but it has to find other outlets—fear of rejection, stage fright, anxiety when driving, etc. Those nagging irrational fears can be faced head-on and conquered. Exposure therapy helps you do this by having you repeatedly face what you fear until you realize it's not scary (Newman, 2016).

Acceptance

Life is unpredictable and full of twists and turns. One day, everything seems to go your way. The next, your car won't start, you spilled coffee on yourself, and your computer crashes. That's just the way it is. It's not fair or balanced. Where you can regain some control is to accept it as it is, spilled coffee and all. When trouble strikes, acknowledge it and figure out if there's a solution. If not, roll with it, and don't beat yourself up over something you can't help.

STRENGTHENING SOCIAL CONNECTIONS

Your social circle is more important than ever when depression strikes. It will break you out of isolation, and that's not only good for your mental health but also your physical health. When you have a healthy social circle, your chances of developing heart disease, stroke, and dementia are cut in half. It helps strengthen your ability to bounce back from stressful situations and decreases your chances of self-harm (C.D.C., 2023).

Even loners need some form of connection. It's another one of those survival instincts from when we were living in tiny tribes or villages, dependent on one another for everything. While independence is a good thing, isolation makes you ill. I'm not saying that you should join a commune. Just stay in touch with your friends and loved ones. Let them know you appreciate them and find new things to bond over. Make a few new friends over shared interests: join a book club, go to a themed convention, or find an online group. The ability to visit in person is the best option, but an online friendship or a weekly phone call to relatives strengthens the bonds. Social bonds are so profound that they can be felt from any distance.

Jess's Story

Jess had a good life. When she wasn't working as a partner in an advertising agency, she was a weekend warrior who loved enjoying the outdoors with her friends. She stayed active and healthy—she ate all the right foods, got plenty of exercise, and had a social calendar that would make a princess jealous.

Everything turned inside out with the outbreak of COVID-19. The world went into lockdown, and Jess's life was confined to her tiny apartment, its walls a prison for the innocent. Her living room used to be a place to throw her gear for the next adventure, and now she felt like she was suffocating in it. She was used to the noise of life, and the silence felt like a pressure chamber. She kept in touch with those she could, using her phone and computer, but they were just harsh reminders of what she could no longer do.

She was a social butterfly, and contact with others was a lifeline that had been yanked away. Sometimes, she would turn on the television or radio only to switch them off. They were filled with reminders. If it wasn't another news report, it was an advertisement featuring the shelter-in-place mandates. A few new shows premiered, and the focus was the pandemic. It was no way to live.

As she felt the symptoms of depression creeping in, she recognized the feelings of loneliness, hopelessness, and difficulty sleeping. She became terrified that the sudden lifestyle change would make her gain weight, so she ate only the bare minimum.

Finally, she had had enough. She decided to force herself out of this rut. She found a good exercise routine online and started right away. She experimented with healthy recipes. She ordered canvas and paint to try a new creative project. For a while, it worked.

Halfway through her painting, she realized tears were running down her cheeks. She hadn't even known she was crying. Each brushstroke led to more tears until she sunk to the floor in desperate sobs. There was no particular reason, so she could do nothing but wait for the tears to stop. By the time she was finally able to get off the floor, she knew that despite her efforts to take care of her depression, she needed professional support.

Though she dreaded it, Jess found a psychologist who specialized in depression and set up a teletherapy session. At first, opening up was hard. She was all about fun and adventure; anything negative was pushed aside. The next session was more accessible, and soon, she understood her despair and the blow the pandemic landed on her mental health. Faced with the truth, she could now begin to make progress.

Jess's psychologist gave her healthy coping strategies to try. They were specific to her needs, and she learned to structure routines, meditate, and work toward realistic goals. It was slow progress, and she was tempted to quit several times, but her determination won. She kept at it and eventually noticed positive changes in her life.

She started having daily video calls with her loved ones. She talked to them about everything, including her feelings. She had never done that before and was surprised at how good it felt. Her connections with them grew more robust, and she no longer feared they would judge her.

While journaling was part of her treatment plan, Jess discovered she had a passion for writing. She vented her emotions through poems and short stories. Words comforted her as they taught her to acknowledge her feelings and needs without judgment.

By the time lockdown lifted, Jess was ready to join the world as someone new. With a deep understanding of her mental health, she had a greater appreciation of life's little pleasures:

- A bird chirping overhead
- A dinner party with close friends
- The love of her family

Jess's story shows how isolation affects your mental health and that asking for help is empowering. She now has the skills to face any challenge, major or minor, head-on.

Nurturing Relationships That Support Mental Health

It's essential to recognize which relationships are good for you and which are toxic. Nurturing a toxic relationship because you're afraid of being alone is worse than being alone. Here are some tips to help you through the process:

- Don't rush into a new relationship or jump to conclusions about an existing one. There's no hurry. Take the time necessary to build trust between both of you.
- Give the other person your full attention when interacting with them. They will notice when your mind is wandering, and they'll also be less engaged. Truly listen when they talk, and they'll follow suit.
- Conversely, don't assume that they won't be interested when you speak. That leads to miscommunication and holding your feelings in.
- Learn the signs of a toxic relationship and steer clear of them.

Healthy relationships support your ability to bounce back after trouble, enhance your coping skills, and decrease your negative frame of mind. Your quality of life and physical body will improve.

PAUSE AND PONDER

Now that you've learned the importance of developing resilience and social connection, here are a few suggestions to help you practice the skills you learned in this chapter.

Resilience Reflection

Reflect on your most recent difficulty. How did you handle it? What could you have done differently? Write these in your journal, and brainstorm strategies to use in the future.

Gratitude Practice

Keep your journal handy because now you'll think of three things to be thankful for this week. Write them down and their positive impressions on your state of mind.

Social Connection Plan

Choose one person you'd like to strengthen your bond with or with whom you'd like to form a new one. Plan out the steps you would take to do so.

SEGUE

Now that you have worked to maintain your mental health, you're ready for the last step in your J.O.U.R.N.E.Y.: Yield enduring change. Here, you will learn to use your new skills to form permanent habits and nurture them for change that lasts the rest of your life.

Y- YIELD ENDURING CHANGE

 "Change is not merely necessary to life—it is life."

— *ALVIN TOFFLER*

THE POSITIVE ASPECTS OF CHANGE

Change can be scary. Leaving it can give you the chills if you've settled into a comfort zone. The comfort zone is your safety net, the familiar territory that encourages you to snuggle up with a fuzzy blanket and ignore the world outside.

It's a trap. Settling into a comfort zone only leads to stagnation. Change is how we evolve in all aspects of our lives. You can't expect a good outcome if you stay where you are forever. Only when you embrace change and try to improve your habits can you see the positive outcomes you desire. Once you see the improvements, you will want to strive for more, and a positive growth cycle will begin, snapping you out of the stagnant one.

If your comfort zone has become a rut, try something new. Pick something that had always sounded interesting, but you needed to be more relaxed (unwilling) to try. Challenge yourself because no one is going to do it for you. Learn to ride a motorcycle, build something with your bare hands and no power tools, or play guitar. The sky's the limit as long as it holds your interest and you've never done it before. You'll gain a new perspective, a sense of accomplishment, and a door out of that rut.

Changing what has become stagnant makes room for new beginnings and beautiful new experiences. You grow as a whole person and bring new wisdom to each new challenge.

Welcoming Change With Open Arms

The ability to adapt to change isn't an inherited gift. It's a skill that can be learned. Big or small, change will happen, and you *can* handle it with grace and determination.

The first thing you need to consider is your frame of mind. Intentionally change it from one of resistance to one of acceptance. Ask yourself what new things will help you in your struggle, and write them down. Brainstorm the pros and cons for each one. Once you've decided to implement one, clearly define your plan so there are minimal surprises. Don't forget your gratitude journal now; it will help strengthen your resolve and overcome setbacks. There will be bumps in the road, but keep your head high. Believe in yourself and trust your intuition.

Mental and Emotional Flexibility

Mental and emotional flexibility are at the core of accepting change. If your mind and heart are rigid, change is a painful process. We adapt to our environment, and if you're stubbornly set in your ways, you risk deterioration instead of adaptation. The trick is to be honest and open-minded and not bother with what you've always thought or how you've always behaved. That is the past, and the present is what matters. I know it's easier said than done, so I've put together a list of tips for staying open and adaptable:

- The mindfulness exercises you learned here will help center you to the present and roll with the punches.
- Be patient. Like everything in this book, it's a work in progress. Give yourself the leeway you need to learn, adapt, and grow.
- It's okay if you need help from your therapist, especially if you've always been resistant.
- The CBT exercises you learned here will be invaluable to learning flexibility since their sole purpose is to revamp your thinking.

FINDING COMFORT IN UNCERTAINTY

The concept of uncertainty can leave a knot of dread in the pit of your stomach. It's an irrational fear of the unknown that hinders your progress. Approaching uncertainty with a sense of curiosity instead of fear will expand your adaptability so you can confidently handle the inevitable changes.

You may be tempted to stomp down all your feelings in uncertain times so you can put on your bravest face. The trick is to ignore this impulse and greet these feelings like an old friend. Yes, you're apprehensive. Yes, you're hopeless. Yes, you have no idea how it will end. After you've accepted that, you can assume that those feelings are temporary if you take steps to make them so. The power is yours to decide what's most essential and pursue that goal.

Lincoln's Story

Lincoln was a passionate political activist with great hopes for the upcoming presidential election. He worked tirelessly for his candidate's campaign, making phone calls, distributing flyers, and organizing fundraisers. He believed this election was an opportunity for his country to start fresh with positive future strategies, and he enthusiastically threw himself into the campaign.

However, Lincoln was devastated when the election didn't go as planned and his candidate lost. Social media only added to his despair, as he couldn't help but scroll through the triumphant posts of his opponents and the sad and angry posts of his party. He lost faith not only in the political system but also in his fellow citizens.

His thoughts grew darker each day, and he became angry and helpless. He cut off contact with his friends and family and lost interest in everything else. His best friend, Landon, tried to reach out to him, but Lincoln refused to talk to him.

Eventually, Landon showed up at Lincoln's door with coffee and doughnuts and refused to leave until Lincoln opened up. Lincoln shared his thoughts and feelings with Landon, who was sympathetic and offered him nonjudgmental advice. Landon urged him to see his therapist, who had helped him through similar challenges.

Lincoln was initially hesitant, but he eventually agreed to make an appointment. His sessions with the therapist were initially challenging, but he found them helpful. The therapist helped him realize that he had tied his identity to his political beliefs and that he needed to separate the two. They developed a plan to channel his disappointment into more constructive outlets.

Lincoln decided to take up activities far removed from politics, such as cycling and volunteering at a soup kitchen. These activities helped him clear his mind and make a positive impact on others. Gradually, he could put everything in perspective and see that politics was just one part of life. Sometimes, you win, and sometimes, you lose, but you can never give up.

CULTIVATING HABITS FOR LASTING CHANGE

I used to think that habits were instinctual, something you did repeatedly without thought. This is only partially correct. You can train yourself to break a bad habit and work to form new habits.

In his article on forming new habits, James Clear (2018) says that the process can be divided into four steps: cue, craving, response, and reward. These steps are more of a never-ending cycle that forms every habit you have.

The cue sends the signal to your brain that a reward is coming. That triggers the craving, so you'll get the reward. First, you have to respond. The response is the habitual action. The reward can be anything that satisfies you (along with a healthy dose of dopamine). Unhealthy habits are easier to form because they usually give you a sense of instant gratification, and that dopamine hit is addictive.

For most, healthy habits (like a new exercise routine) are more difficult because the reward takes longer to feel. Try triggering the reward afterward to help you form a new, healthy habit to replace an unhealthy one. For example, if you're on a diet craving junk food, replace it with a piece of fruit or something else you like but is better for you. You could also distract yourself from the craving by doing something satisfying else—calling your mom, for example. The possibilities are endless if you know how to hack the habit system.

Practical Steps for Habit Formation

Following this formula will set you up for success when building or replacing new habits. It can be tedious, but these steps make it much easier and more rewarding.

Choose One Habit

While getting comfortable with the process, choose one habit you'd like to adopt. Be clear on precisely what you want to accomplish. For example, you want to take walks in the morning before you start your day but can never get out of bed on time.

Make a List

Listing the habits you already have that revolve around the habit you want to form will tell you what you should change. For example, in the morning walk example, you could list your habits of staying up too late, eating too soon before bed, and pushing the snooze button on the alarm.

Brainstorm

If you try to stop a habit cold, you're depriving yourself of the reward you crave. The best way to ensure your success is to substitute the bad habit for a better one. For example, you could try relaxing yoga or meditation instead of a bedtime snack.

Journal Your Progress

Check-in with yourself at the end of the day. Ensure you're meeting your own expectations and adjust your goals if needed.

Don't Get Discouraged

By tracking your progress, you'll see that things don't always go according to plan. This is where you'll be tested. You will be tempted to give up, but don't! It's a temporary setback, and tomorrow is a new day.

It May Take Several Tries

Building new habits is an exercise of repetition. Don't be surprised if you slide back into your old habits more than once before you're finally successful. It's frustrating, but it's worth it. *You're* worth it. Planning for the eventualities will quiet most of the frustration since you'll already know how to forge ahead.

Make Your New Habits Stick

The most obvious advice for this is to stay consistent. That little word makes it sound so easy, but habits are automatic. To build new ones or replace old ones, you have to override your automatic responses with intentional ones.

For one month, set reminders for yourself to practice your new habit. Your phone is ideal for this since you most likely always have it on you. You can set as many alarms as you need to keep you accountable. If you don't have a phone or prefer another method, write it in your hand or place notes all over your house. As long as it remains prominent in your mind, whichever method you choose will help.

You may enlist the help of a friend as an accountability partner. You could make a game of it if friendly competition motivates you. You could also find an online group dedicated to the same goal and use that as a support system.

No matter what, remember that nobody is perfect. It's okay to slip up, backslide, and get frustrated. As long as you don't give up, you can't fail.

Maria's Story

Maria was a busy single mom with two jobs. She had been doing teletherapy sessions for her depression, but her life was so hectic that she couldn't see any difference. In between getting up much too early to get her and her eight-year-old daughter ready for the day, working for eight hours at a convenience store, taking her daughter to the babysitter after school to work for five more hours as a private caregiver in the evening; and then picking up her daughter, getting dinner ready, cleaning, and nightly rituals; she was too exhausted to put in as much effort as she knew she should.

On a rare full day off, Maria dropped her daughter off for a sleep-over party and made a phone call that changed her life. She booked a special session with her therapist and opened up about everything she was going through. She always felt rushed during the other appointments, held back so her daughter wouldn't overhear, or was distracted by doing chores simultaneously. This time, she sat down and let it all out.

The therapist's first suggestion was to slow down. That confused Maria. How was she supposed to slow down with a kid and two jobs? She had been running at full speed for so many years that she didn't know where to begin. The therapist gave her a list of things to do every day. She was ordered to make time for them (nicely, of course). She was prescribed yoga and journaling before bed to start. Though she was exhausted, she made the effort. She couldn't let her daughter see her like that.

She added mindfulness, affirmations, and meditation to her daily rituals. It wasn't easy, and she forgot sometimes, but eventually, it became second nature. She could fully bring herself to the present and slow down the chaos of her mind. She could stop and enjoy her child's company instead of constantly thinking about what must be done. She was still busy, but it didn't seem so over-whelming now.

Maria felt embarrassed when the therapist made her next sugges-tion. She was embarrassed because it was apparent, and had never thought of it before. Maria had experience in two fields. Indeed, she could find one job that covered the bills. It took a lot of work and training, but she finally qualified as a certified nurse's aide (CNA). Now, she's working on her nursing degree. With her new habits to help her, she only needs her therapist for the occasional check-in. She and her daughter now do yoga together, a bonding experience that will last their lifetimes.

PAUSE AND PONDER

You now have the skills to make your efforts result in lasting change for the better. Here are some suggestions to set you up for success.

Change Reflection

Write about a recent change in your life. How did you adapt to it? What did you learn about yourself?

Habit Formation Plan

Choose a new positive habit you want to develop. Make a detailed plan for integrating it into your daily life.

Resilience Story

In a tiny village nestled between snow-dusted mountains, young Oliver learned the true meaning of resilience, not through victory but through relentless perseverance against the shadows of depression that clouded his young mind.

Once a cheerful child, Oliver found his world dimming as an inexplicable sadness took hold of him early in his adolescence. His legs, already weakened by a disease in infancy, seemed to symbolize the further restrictions he felt mentally, trapping him in a cycle of isolation and despair. Despite this, he found a flicker of joy in watching birds—symbols of the freedom he craved, both physically and emotionally.

His father, noticing the fleeting sparks of happiness in Oliver's eyes when he watched the birds, crafted him a kite painted like a bright bluebird. It was more than a gift; it was a lifeline, a way for Oliver to connect with the skies he admired.

Every afternoon, despite the weight of his emotions, Oliver would wheel himself to the grassy hill at the edge of the village. With the kite in hand, he felt his spirits lift slightly as he watched it soar. With its open view of the horizon, the hill became his refuge, where he could breathe a little easier and feel lighter.

One day, a group of children approached him, including a boy named Marcus. They observed his solitary ritual with a mix of curiosity and pity.

"Why do you come here every day?" Marcus asked, not fully grasping the depth of Oliver's struggle.

"Because one day, I will make this kite fly higher than anyone else's," Oliver replied with a gentle determination, his eyes never leaving the bluebird in the sky.

The children laughed, not understanding that for Oliver, the kite was more than a game; it was a battle against his inner demons, a way to pull himself out of the darkness that often enveloped him.

Seasons changed, and Oliver's mastery over the kite grew alongside a gradual improvement in his mood. He learned to harness the wind, his only companion on the hill, who seemed to understand his silent pleas for strength. Through this connection, Oliver found therapy in the rhythms of nature, slowly stitching the frayed edges of his spirit back together.

When the village organized its annual kite festival, Oliver joined with a heart of quiet hope. His bluebird kite, now a symbol of his journey through depression, danced in the sky with a vigor that surprised the onlookers.

Marcus's kite, a giant, impressive eagle, took an early lead. Still, as the wind grew stronger, Oliver's intimate understanding of its patterns allowed him to maneuver his kite exceptionally. To the astonishment of all, the bluebird rose higher and higher, eventually outpacing all others.

As the festival ended and Oliver's kite remained the highest in the sky, Marcus approached him, a newfound respect in his eyes. "You were right," he conceded. "You do speak the wind's language."

Oliver smiled a genuine smile that reached his eyes for the first time in years. "Sometimes, you don't need to run to touch the sky. You just need to ask the wind for a dance."

Years later, the village still told the story of Oliver and his bluebird kite. It had become a tale not just of overcoming physical limitations but of battling and conquering the more profound, invisible struggles of depression. Oliver's story taught them that sometimes, the greatest strength lies in the quiet persistence to rise above one's inner storms and find joy by letting a kite soar.

Think of a tough time in your life when you showed resilience. What did it teach you? How did it shape your approach to challenges?

SEGUE

This is the last step in your J.O.U.R.N.E.Y.

Of course, the mental health recovery journey is ongoing, but the skills you've learned here will make the road smoother. You can use these strategies to grow and thrive for the rest of your life. You are not alone. You are strong. You can succeed.

Before You Go

As you take the final steps of your J.O.U.R.N.E.Y. through this book, I hope your arsenal is filled with a host of activities to help you learn more about yourself and the most effective ways to reduce the impact of depression on your life. There are a host of activities within these pages to keep you active... from reflecting on the many inspiring stories I've shared to writing a new entry in your diary, trying out a few mindfulness pursuits, and answering self-assessment checklists. If this information has helped you see the many ways in which your daily choices impact your mental health and well-being, then I hope you can leave a few words to help someone who is struggling to move past the clutches of depression.

TAKE A MOMENT TO SHARE YOUR THOUGHTS!

Thanks for your support. We are at our bravest and best when we take the time to help someone else, even as we work to help ourselves.

Scan the QR code below

CONCLUSION

The end of every journey is the beginning of a new one. It is my dream to help anyone who reads this book to take back their life and break the cycle of depression. I see you. Sometimes, it feels like you're on a speeding train with no power to stop it. Now, you have the skills to control a condition that takes on a life of its own if left unchecked. Each new exercise you incorporate into your routine is a concrete step to rise above your depression so you can grab onto the hope that I offer. The work can be overwhelming, but I promise it's worth it if you put in the time.

Your new understanding and self-awareness give you an edge that you didn't have before. You've learned that the enemy is not yourself but the illness that has taken control of you. Now you know that it's okay to try new and unconventional ways to support your mental health. Depression is like a demon from a movie, taking possession and forcing you to say, feel, and do things that are not good for you. With the sheer force of your will, this guide is your exorcism. With it, you reclaim peace and confidence over your mind and body. Your fight with depression is like a battle in reverse. Instead of overpowering the enemy with brute force and violence, you wash it over with a wave of hope and optimism.

Some are so used to their negative mind that they don't want to improve. You've proven otherwise by finishing this book and are stubborn enough to get through the hard times. You want permanent change, and your determination will ensure that it happens.

I want to share one more story with you before we say goodbye.

MY STORY

I struggled with depression most of my life. I had lofty dreams in school. I knew who I wanted to be and where I wanted to go. What I never thought about was how I was going to get there. I never made plans, only daydreaming as I procrastinated on my homework. When school was over and I was thrust into the real world, I found out that life was more challenging than I ever imagined.

I struggled to make ends meet, and my mind struggled against feelings of failure and shattered dreams. I knew I was depressed. For years, I thought I *deserved* to be miserable. I pushed everyone away, thinking it would be easier if they hated me. I wasn't exactly thinking about hurting myself, but I did seriously consider disappearing on the Appalachian trail or something equally dramatic.

A mother's intuition saved me. She unexpectedly arrived at my door before sunrise as I prepared to leave. She and my dad lived 600 miles away, so the long drive was a hassle. She always informed me when she was coming in case of an emergency, so I was surprised by her unexpected visit. When she saw my suitcase by the couch, I could tell by the look on her face that she knew what I was planning. We sat on the sofa, and she silently held my hand until I was ready to talk. I broke down in tears and told her everything. She hugged me and let me cry it out. When I stopped crying, she looked me in the eye.

What she said was not what I had expected. As she shared her experiences from before my birth, I was horrified by the abuses she had endured. They were far worse than I had ever imagined. However, I sensed that her intention was not to diminish my struggles but to share her story and help me understand her challenges.

She told me that talking about such things in her generation was highly discouraged, forcing people to push it down and pretend it never happened. It wasn't until she moved out of the house that she sought help for her depression and post-traumatic stress disorder (P.T.S.D.). She urged me to do the same before I did something drastic. I promised her, and she stayed with me for two months to ensure I kept my word. She was there after each session to comfort me through the inevitable breakdowns. After a week, the breakdowns stopped, and I began the process of coping on my own. The rest of the time was spent having a good time and reminiscing.

Thanks to her and my new therapist, I began my own J.O.U.R.N.E.Y. I won't lie; sometimes I still struggle, but now I know that I'm loved and supported, and I have more good days than bad. Soon, you will too.

I hope you will carry the wisdom you've learned in these pages into every day of your life. Remember, your journey to a healthier, happier you constantly evolves, and you have the power to shape it.

If you found the methods here helpful, please leave a review so that others in need may find it. To your health!

REFERENCES

A Little Dose of Happy. (2023, April 20). *11 Habits for Cultivating Gratitude (Even in Hard Times)*. A Little Dose of Happy. https://aldohappy.com/cultivating-gratitude

Ackerman, C. (2018, February 12). *CBT's Cognitive Restructuring (CR) For Tackling Cognitive Distortions*. PositivePsychology.com. https://positivepsychology.com/cbt-cognitive-restructuring-cognitive-distortions/

Advanced Psychiatry Associates. (2019, August 12). *How Anxiety & Depression Impacts Your Physical Health*. Advanced Psychiatry Associates. https://advancedpsychiatryassociates.com/resources/blog/the-effects-of-anxiety-and-depression-on-your-physical-health/

American Psychological Association. (2016, May 17). *10 Tips to Build Resilience*. Psych Central. https://psychcentral.com/lib/10-tips-to-build-resilience#1

Anahana. (2021, July 26). *Yoga Nidra For Beginners: Calmness From an Easy Sleep Meditation*. Www.anahana.com. https://www.anahana.com/en/wellbeing-blog/yoga/yoga-nidra-for-beginners

Anahana. (2024, January 19). *How 7 Amazing Yoga Nidra Benefits Can Help - You May Be Surprised*. Www.anahana.com. https://www.anahana.com/en/wellbeing-blog/yoga/benefits-yoga-nidra

Andreu, Maria E.. *I Wanna See You Brave*. Maria E. Andreu. August 5, 2016. https://mariaeandreu.com/2016/08/05/wanna-see-brave/

Ascend Float Spa. (2020, January 9). *3 Ways Floatation Therapy Can Help With Depression - Ascend Float Spa 3 Ways Floatation Therapy Can Help With Depression*. Ascend Float Spa. https://ascendfloatspa.com/3-ways-floatation-therapy-can-help-with-depression/

Astorino, D. (2023, April 19). *5 Health Benefits of Spending Time in Nature*. Www.onemedical.com. https://www.onemedical.com/blog/healthy-living/health-benefits-nature/

Avril, B. (2024, February 20). *Mental Health Check-Ins And Why They're Important*. Therapy with Empathy. https://www.therapywithempathy.com/blog/mental-health-check-ins-and-why-theyre-important

B.C.B, R. M., Psy D. (2015, November 1). *How Biofeedback Reduces Anxiety, Depression and Certain Medical Conditions*. Evolutions Behavioral Health Services. https://www.evolutionsbh.com/articles/how-biofeedback-reduces-anxiety-depression-and-stress-related-medical-conditions/

Bailey, A. (2022). *What Are Coping Mechanisms?* Verywell Health. https://www.very wellhealth.com/coping-mechanisms-5272135

Bailey, S.-L. (2016, October 5). *How To Change Your Unhealthy Coping Mechanisms.* Life in a Break Down. https://www.lifeinabreakdown.com/change-unhealthy-coping-mechanisms/

Baton Rouge Behavioral Hospital. (2020, December 23). *Replacing Unhealthy Coping Mechanisms in 2021 - Baton Rouge BH.* Baton Rouge Behavioral Hospital. https://batonrougebehavioral.com/replacing-unhealthy-coping-mechanisms-in-2021/

Baulch, J. (2019, March 14). *Self-Awareness: The Key to Mental Health & Wellbeing.* Inner Melbourne Psychology. https://www.innermelbpsychology.com.au/self-awareness-mental-health/

Baylor Scott & White Health. (2020, March 31). *19 quick and easy mood-boosting activities.* Www.bswhealth.com. https://www.bswhealth.com/blog/19-quick-and-easy-mood-boosting-activities

Beautifully Simply You. (2018, December 17). *There is Growth in Change.* Beautifully Simply You. https://beautifullysimplyyou.com/2018/12/17/there-is-growth-in-change/

Bernstein, S. (2023, March 13). *Depression vs. Sadness: When Should You See a Doctor?* WebMD. https://www.webmd.com/depression/depression-sadness

Better Health Channel. (2022, February 24). *Strong relationships, strong health.* Better Health Channel. https://www.betterhealth.vic.gov.au/health/HealthyLiving/Strong-relationships-strong-health

BetterHelp Editorial Team. (2024, March 29). *What's Expressive Arts Therapy? | BetterHelp.* Www.betterhelp.com. https://www.betterhelp.com/advice/therapy/what-is-expressive-therapy-and-when-is-it-used/

Beyond Blue. (2022). *Causes of depression - Beyond Blue.* Www.beyondblue.org.au. https://www.beyondblue.org.au/mental-health/depression/causes-of-depression

Bjur, B. (2012). Burn's Depression Checklist. In *University of Wisconsin Green Bay.* University of Wisconsin . https://www.uwgb.edu/UWGBCMS/media/Continueing-Professional-Education/files/Assess-Pkt-1-Burns-Depression-Checklist.pdf

Borchard, T. (2017, November 14). *10 Foods I Eat Every Day to Beat Depression.* EverydayHealth.com. https://www.everydayhealth.com/columns/therese-borchard-sanity-break/foods-eat-every-day-beat-depression/

Boudin, PsyD, M. (2023, April 5). *41 Journal Prompts for Depression.* Choosing Therapy. https://www.choosingtherapy.com/journal-prompts-for-depression/

Bradley, J. (2023, July 5). *Embracing Uncertainty: Navigating Change for Personal Growth and Transformation.* Lampshade of ILLUMINATION. https://medium.

com/lampshade-of-illumination/embracing-uncertainty-navigating-change-for-personal-growth-and-transformation-862032c56c0b

Brainy Quote. (2001). *Alvin Toffler Quotes*. Brainy Quote. https://www.brainyquote.com/quotes/alvin_toffler_404980

Bridges, F. (2019, February 5). *Five Ways to Make a Habit Stick*. Forbes. https://www.forbes.com/sites/francesbridges/2019/02/25/five-ways-to-make-a-habit-stick/?sh=1835583c135b

Bruce, D. F. (2023, April 25). *Causes of Depression*. WebMD. https://www.webmd.com/depression/causes-depression

Bruce, D. F., & PhD. (2023, July 17). *Diet and Depression*. WebMD. https://www.webmd.com/depression/diet-recovery

Burton, K. (2019, December 30). *Ellie's Story: Therapy Dogs Help Heal*. Paws & Think. https://www.pawsandthink.org/ellies-story-therapy-dogs-help-heal/

Calmer. (2020, December 16). *How to practise self-reflection*. Calmer. https://www.thisiscalmer.com/blog/how-to-practise-self-reflection

Campbell, M. (2018, July 12). *Change is a sign of growth*. Struggling Forward. https://medium.com/struggle-first-thrive-later/change-is-a-sign-of-growth-242ef5c9b638

Carter, Ph.D., C. (2020, October 21). *7 strategies to help you live with uncertainty*. Ideas.ted.com. https://ideas.ted.com/7-strategies-to-help-you-live-with-uncertainty/

Cartreine, J. (2016, May 6). *More than sad: Depression affects your ability to think - Harvard Health Blog*. Harvard Health Blog. https://www.health.harvard.edu/blog/sad-depression-affects-ability-think-201605069551

Cassata, C. (2021, May 20). *How Depression Affects Relationships and Tips to Help*. Psych Central. https://psychcentral.com/depression/how-depression-affects-relationships

CDC. (2023, March 30). *How Does Social Connectedness Affect Health?* Centers for Disease Control and Prevention. https://www.cdc.gov/emotional-wellbeing/social-connectedness/affect-health.htm

Celestine Ph.D, N. (2017, January 26). *The Science of Happiness in Positive Psychology 101*. PositivePsychology.com. https://positivepsychology.com/happiness/#definition-happiness

Centers for Disease Control and Prevention. (2023, August 23). *Sadness and Depression | How Right Now | Centers for Disease Control and Prevention*. Www.cdc.gov. https://www.cdc.gov/howrightnow/emotion/sadness/index.html

Centre for Optimism. (2023). *What is Optimism?* Www.centreforoptimism.com. https://www.centreforoptimism.com/whatisoptimism

Chang, Y.-H., Yang, C.-T., & Hsieh, S. (2023). Social support enhances the mediating effect of psychological resilience on the relationship between life satisfaction and depressive symptom severity. *Scientific Reports, 13*(1). https://doi.org/10.1038/s41598-023-31863-7

Cherry, K. (2011, May 21). *What Is Biofeedback and How Does It Work?* Verywell Mind; Verywell Mind. https://www.verywellmind.com/what-is-biofeedback-2794875

Cherry, K. (2021, August 19). *What Is Expressive Arts Therapy?* Verywell Mind. https://www.verywellmind.com/expressive-arts-therapy-definition-types-techniques-and-efficacy-5197564

Cherry, K. (2022a, September 2). *What are the benefits of mindfulness?* Verywell Mind. https://www.verywellmind.com/the-benefits-of-mindfulness-5205137

Cherry, K. (2022b, October 6). *10 Ways to Improve Your Resilience.* Verywell Mind. https://www.verywellmind.com/ways-to-become-more-resilient-2795063

Cherry, K. (2023, March 10). *What Is Self-Awareness?* Verywell Mind. https://www.verywellmind.com/what-is-self-awareness-2795023

Clear, J. (2018). *How to start new habits that actually stick.* James Clear. https://jamesclear.com/three-steps-habit-change

Cleveland Clinic. (2020a, September 13). *What Is Yoga Nidra?* Cleveland Clinic. https://health.clevelandclinic.org/what-is-yoga-nidra

Cleveland Clinic. (2020b, December 21). *Biofeedback: What Is It & Procedure Details.* Cleveland Clinic. https://my.clevelandclinic.org/health/treatments/13354-biofeedback

Cleveland Clinic. (2021a, November 23). *4 Reasons to Do a Digital Detox.* Cleveland Clinic. https://health.clevelandclinic.org/digital-detox

Cleveland Clinic. (2021b, December 1). *How Light Therapy Can Help With Seasonal Affective Disorder (SAD).* Cleveland Clinic. https://health.clevelandclinic.org/light-therapy

Coaching, C. H. (2019, July 2). *10 Ways to Embrace Change and Become More You.* Courtney Harris Coaching. https://courtneyharriscoaching.com/how-to-embrace-change-and-become-more-you/

Cognitive Behavioral Therapy Los Angeles. (2020). *Cognitive Behavioral Therapy Exercises.* Cognitive Behavioral Therapy Los Angeles. https://cogbtherapy.com/cognitive-behavioral-therapy-exercises

Corliss, J. (2022, October 28). *Light therapy: Not just for seasonal depression?* Harvard Health. https://www.health.harvard.edu/blog/light-therapy-not-just-for-seasonal-depression-202210282840

Cozy Simple Calm. (2019, October 7). *Celebrating the simple pleasures in life.* Cozy. Simple. Calm. https://cozysimplecalm.com/celebrating-the-simple-pleasures-in-life/

D'Amico, P. (2017, December 28). *How Positive Thoughts Can Benefit Your Mental health - PM.* Paradigm Treatment. https://paradigmtreatment.com/positive-thoughts-benefit-mental-health/

Davis, Ph.D., T. (2021, May 19). *9 Ways to Cultivate a Positive Mindset | Psychology Today.* Www.psychologytoday.com. https://www.psychologytoday.com/us/blog/click-here-happiness/202105/9-ways-cultivate-positive-mindset

Davis, D. M., & Hayes, J. A. (2012, July). What are the benefits of mindfulness? *American Psychological Association.* https://www.apa.org/monitor/2012/07-08/ce-corner

Davis, F. (2022, May 19). *How to Be Open-Minded: 10 Tips to Help You Grow & Explore Life.* Faith M. Davis. https://faithmdavis.com/blog/how-to-be-open-minded

Davis-Baird, B. (2023, October 9). *7 Amazing Benefits of Yoga Nidra.* YogaUOnline. https://yogauonline.com/yoga-health-benefits/yoga-for-stress-relief/7-amazing-benefits-of-yoga-nidra/

Daze, G. (2022, August 1). *Virtual Reality (VR) and Depression Treatment.* BrainsWay. https://www.brainsway.com/knowledge-center/virtual-reality-and-depression/

Depoy, A. (2020, May 3). *The Mental Health Benefits of Gratitude.* Www.nationwidechildrens.org. https://www.nationwidechildrens.org/family-resources-education/700childrens/2020/05/gratitude

Dibdin, E. (2021, December 17). *How to Connect with Joy and Happiness When You Have Depression.* Psych Central. https://psychcentral.com/depression/happy-when-depressed

Dimitratos, S. (2018, October 1). *Food and Mood: What Is Nutritional Psychiatry?* American Society for Nutrition. https://nutrition.org/food-and-mood-what-is-nutritional-psychiatry/

Dodgen-Magee, Psy.D., D. (2022, March 15). *Psychological Flexibility: How to Face Change and Unknowns | Psychology Today.* Www.psychologytoday.com. https://www.psychologytoday.com/us/blog/deviced/202203/psychological-flexibility-how-face-change-and-unknowns

Eatough, E. (2021, August 23). *Seeking help for your mental health is brave. And beneficial.* Www.betterup.com. https://www.betterup.com/blog/seeking-help

Eikanas, M. (2023, January 11). *Surviving the Ups & Downs of Life.* Lead Life Well. https://leadlifewell.com/blog/surviving-the-ups-downs-of-life/

Eisenberg Family Depression Center. (2024). *Self-assessment tools | Eisenberg Family Depression Center.* Depressioncenter.org. https://depressioncenter.org/outreach-education/depression-toolkit/looking-more-resources/self-assessment-tools

Elara. (2018, August 13). *VR for Depression - Virtual Reality Therapy for Depression*. Elara. https://elarasystems.com/vr-helps-depression/

Elmer, J. (2021, October 22). *When Depression Lies: Cognitive Distortions*. Psych Central. https://psychcentral.com/depression/cognitive-distortions-the-lies-depression-tells

eSoft Skills Team. (2023, December 19). *Embrace Change with Psychological Flexibility*. ESoft Skills. https://esoftskills.com/psychological-flexibility/

Ferguson, S. (2022, August 15). *Mindfulness For Depression: Tips And Exercises*. Psych Central. https://psychcentral.com/depression/how-does-mindfulness-reduce-depression

Find Your Words. (2020). *Depression Test - Online Self-Assessment*. Find Your Words. https://findyourwords.org/self-care/depression-assessment-tool/

Fitzgerald, J. (2019, January 22). *Depression versus sadness: How to tell the difference*. Www.medicalnewstoday.com. https://www.medicalnewstoday.com/articles/314418

Foothills at Red Oak Recovery. (2022, February 25). *3 Tips for Overcoming Depression Triggers*. Foothills at Red Oak Recovery. https://foothillsatredoak.com/teen-recovery-blog/3-tips-for-overcoming-depression-triggers/

Fotuhi, M. (2020, January 9). *Neurofeedback for Depression and Anxiety Treatment*. NeuroGrow. https://neurogrow.com/biofeedback-treatment-for-anxiety-and-depression/

Friedman, D. (2022, September 13). *Your Totally Manageable, 10-Step Guide to Doing a Digital Detox*. Health.com. https://www.health.com/mind-body/digital-detox

Full Spectrum Solutions. (n.d.). *Light Box Testimonials*. Full Spectrum Solutions. Retrieved April 3, 2024, from https://www.fullspectrumsolutions.com/pages/testimonials-light-therapy

Gabi. (2023). *Gabi's story: my struggle with speaking up about my depression and loneliness*. Www.mentalhealth.org.uk. https://www.mentalhealth.org.uk/explore-mental-health/stories/gabis-story-struggle-speaking-about-my-depression-and-loneliness

Gabriel. (2023, February 20). *Mental Health Matters: Importance Of Seeking Professional Help*. Https://Peaceofmind4wellness.com/. https://peaceofmind4wellness.com/mental-health-matters-the-importance-of-seeking-professional-help/

Gejsek, D. (2020). *Virtual Reality Therapy*. Circuitstream.com. https://circuitstream.com/blog/virtual-reality-therapy

Gillette, H. (2014, November 21). *41 Journal Prompts to Cope with Depression Symptoms*. Psych Central. https://psychcentral.com/depression/journal-prompts-for-depression#prompts-for-sadness

Giorgi, A. (2013). *Pet Therapy | Definition and Patient Education*. Healthline. https://www.healthline.com/health/pet-therapy

Goldman, L. (2019). *Depression: What it is, symptoms, causes, treatment, types, and more*. Www.medicalnewstoday.com. https://www.medicalnewstoday.com/articles/8933

Goodreads. (n.d.-a). *A quote by Dan Millman*. Www.goodreads.com. Retrieved April 8, 2024, from https://www.goodreads.com/quotes/10158365-you-don-t-have-to-control-your-thoughts-you-just-have

Goodreads. (n.d.-b). *A quote from Les Misérables*. Www.goodreads.com. Retrieved April 11, 2024, from https://www.goodreads.com/quotes/10095-even-the-darkest-night-will-end-and-the-sun-will

GoodTherapy. (2018, September 26). *Coping Mechanisms*. GoodTherapy.org Therapy Blog. https://www.goodtherapy.org/blog/psychpedia/coping-mechanisms

Gopinath, P. (2023, September 28). *The Power of Consistency - How One Good Habit Can Transform Your Life*. Www.linkedin.com. https://www.linkedin.com/pulse/power-consistency-how-one-good-habit-can-transform-your-gopinath

Gotter, A., & Caplain, E. (2016, November 22). *Everything You Need to Know About Getting Help for Depression*. Healthline. https://www.healthline.com/health/depression/help-for-depression#treatment-plans

Greer, J. (2022, October 13). *Why Change Is Important for Your Mental Health*. Eugene Therapy. https://eugenetherapy.com/article/why-change-is-important-for-your-mental-health/

Gruman-Bender, R. (2013, December 9). *Expressive Therapy for Depression*. Healthline. https://www.healthline.com/health/depression/expressive-therapy

Gupta, S. (2023, May 26). *The Importance of Self-Reflection: How Looking Inward Can Improve Your Mental Health*. Verywell Mind. https://www.verywellmind.com/self-reflection-importance-benefits-and-strategies-7500858

Hagen, A. (2020, June 24). *5 Steps to Embrace Uncertainty*. Psych Central. https://psychcentral.com/blog/learning-to-embrace-uncertainty

Hanson-Baiden, B.Sc. , J. (2022, January 18). *What is Nutritional Psychiatry?* News-Medical.net. https://www.news-medical.net/health/What-is-Nutritional-Psychiatry.aspx

Happify. (2022). *What Is the Science of Happiness?* Happify.com; Twill. https://www.happify.com/hd/what-is-the-science-of-happiness/

Harmony. (2021, June 16). *Tips for Cultivating a Positive Mindset*. Harmony. https://www.grwhealth.com/post/tips-for-cultivating-a-positive-mindset/

Hartney, E. (2020). *10 Cognitive Distortions That Can Lead to Addiction Relapse*. Verywell Mind. https://www.verywellmind.com/ten-cognitive-distortions-identified-in-cbt-22412

Harvard Health. (2019, March 21). *Benefits of mindfulness*. HelpGuide.org. https://www.helpguide.org/harvard/benefits-of-mindfulness.htm

HCA Florida Healthcare. (2022, September 25). *5 foods that help fight depression | HCA Florida*. Www.hcafloridahealthcare.com. https://www.hcafloridahealthcare.com/healthy-living/blog/5-foods-that-help-fight-depression

Henderson, L. (2023, January 16). *Five tips to make new habits stick | blog - Heart Foundation*. Www.heartfoundation.org.nz. https://www.heartfoundation.org.nz/about-us/news/blogs/five-tips-to-make-new-habits-stick

Henning, Z. (2023, October 23). *Recovery is not linear*. The Bear Facts. https://lcmbearfacts.com/19348/opinions/recovery-is-not-linear/

Hollimon, N. (2020, August 3). *What Is Expressive Therapy?* WebMD. https://www.webmd.com/mental-health/expressive-therapy

Hoshaw, C. (2022, March 29). *What is mindfulness? A simple practice for greater well-being*. Healthline. https://www.healthline.com/health/mind-body/what-is-mindfulness

Hunnicutt, C. (2014, June 25). *Animal Assisted Therapy: Personal Stories of Therapeutic Success*. Rosewood Centers for Eating Disorders. https://www.rosewoodranch.com/animal-assisted-therapy-personal-stories-of-therapeutic-success/

Husson University. (2022, July 20). *The Healing Power of Animals: Benefits of Animal-Assisted Therapy*. Husson University. https://www.husson.edu/online/blog/2022/07/benefits-of-animal-assisted-therapy

Imoore. (2007, June 20). *Beck's Depression Inventory*. Https://Www.ismanet.org/Doctoryourspirit/Pdfs/Beck-Depression-Inventory-BDI.pdf ; ISMA. https://www.ismanet.org/doctoryourspirit/pdfs/Beck-Depression-Inventory-BDI.pdf

Intelligent Change. (2024). *How to Embrace Change in Your Life*. Intelligent Change. https://www.intelligentchange.com/blogs/read/how-to-embrace-change-in-your-life

Jeffs, L. (2019, December 30). *How to Improve Your Self Awareness? - Lisa Jeffs*. Lisajeffs.com. https://lisajeffs.com/how-to-improve-your-self-awareness/

Johnson, B. (2020, April 29). *Depression Versus Sadness: When to Talk with your Doctor*. Find a DO | Doctors of Osteopathic Medicine. https://findado.osteopathic.org/depression-versus-sadness-when-to-talk-with-your-doctor

Johnson, J. (2019, August 20). *What foods are good for helping depression?* Medicalnewstoday.com; Medical News Today. https://www.medicalnewstoday.com/articles/318428

Johnson, J. (2020, July 10). *Animal therapy: How it works, benefits, and more*. Www.medicalnewstoday.com. https://www.medicalnewstoday.com/articles/animal-therapy

Julia. (2023, February 22). *5 Reasons To Do A Digital Detox*. Cardinal Clinic. https:// cardinalclinic.co.uk/5-reasons-to-do-a-digital-detox/

Kalin, N. H. (2019). Developing Innovative and Novel Treatment Strategies. *American Journal of Psychiatry, 176*(11), 885–887. https://doi.org/10.1176/appi. ajp.2019.19090952

Krause, N. (2022, May 11). *45 Quick Mood Boosting Activities to Lift Your Spirits*. Happier Human. https://www.happierhuman.com/mood-boosting-activities/

Kripalu Center for Yoga and Health. (2024). *Four Ways to Cultivate Optimism*. Kripalu. https://kripalu.org/resources/four-ways-cultivate-optimism

Kruglanski, A. (2023, December 20). *How to embrace uncertainty | Psyche Guides*. Psyche. https://psyche.co/guides/how-to-face-uncertain-situations-and-embrace-opportunity

Krysus Human Performance. (2022, July 13). *How to Prepare For a Float Session | Float Tank and Therapy Tips for First Timers*. Krysus. https://www.krysushp. com/learn/how-to-prepare-for-a-float-session/

Kunst, Ph.D., J. (2014, December 17). *7 Strategies to Face Life's Challenges*. Psychology Today. https://www.psychologytoday.com/us/blog/head shrinkers-guide-the-galaxy/201412/7-strategies-face-lifes-challenges

Lambert, N. M., Fincham, F. D., & Stillman, T. F. (2012). Gratitude and depressive symptoms: The role of positive reframing and positive emotion. *Cognition & Emotion, 26*(4), 615–633. https://doi.org/10.1080/02699931.2011.595393

Lancia, G. (2022, March 18). *28 Inspiring Mental Health Quotes That Will Empower You*. PositivePsychology.com. https://positivepsychology.com/mental-health-quotes/

Laurence, E. (2022, August 11). *Virtual Reality Therapy: Everything You Need To Know*. Forbes Health. https://www.forbes.com/health/mind/virtual-reality-therapy/

Lawson, MD, K. (2024). *Nurture Your Relationships*. Taking Charge of Your Health & Wellbeing. https://www.takingcharge.csh.umn.edu/nurture-your-relationships

Lebow, H. (2014, September 27). *5 Tips to Help You Adapt to Change*. Psych Central. https://psychcentral.com/blog/adapting-to-change#tips

Legg, T. (2015). *9 Depression Symptoms to Look Out For*. Healthline. https://www. healthline.com/health/depression/recognizing-symptoms

Lewine, L. (2020, February 10). *"I Tried Float Therapy And Forgot What It Felt Like To Be Stressed Out."* Women's Health. https://www.womenshealthmag.com/health/ a30754055/float-therapy-sensory-deprivation/

Lifeline Support Toolkit. (n.d.). *How to do a digital detox*. Lifeline Support Toolkit. Retrieved April 5, 2024, from https://toolkit.lifeline.org.au/articles/tech niques/how-to-do-a-digital-detox

Lloydspharmacy Online Doctor. (2015, September 22). *Do I Have Depression? | LloydsPharmacy Online Doctor UK.* Onlinedoctor.lloydspharmacy.com. https://onlinedoctor.lloydspharmacy.com/uk/mental-health-and-wellbeing-advice/do-i-have-depression

Lovering, C. (2022, February 28). *7 Best Relaxation Exercises: Meditation, Grounding, and More.* Psych Central. https://psychcentral.com/lib/relaxation-exercises-and-techniques

Lukin, D. K. (2016, September 8). *Cognitive Behavioral Therapy Exercises.* Lukin Center for Psychotherapy. https://www.lukincenter.com/5-surprisingly-effective-cognitive-behavioral-therapy-exercises/

Lundbeck. (2023). *MDD Connection | Depression and Social Life.* MDDCA. https://www.mddconnection.com/depression-and-social-life

Mane, S. (2023, February 27). *10 Ways to Overcome Challenges in Life* 🎯 . Www.linkedin.com. https://www.linkedin.com/pulse/10-ways-overcome-challenges-life-satish-s-mane-

Mann, D. (2012, May 9). *How to Manage Depression Triggers.* WebMD; WebMD. https://www.webmd.com/depression/features/depression-triggers

Manwaring, J. (2022, October 3). *Why Is Being Self-Aware Important for Your Mental Health? - San Diego | API.* Alvarado Parkway Institute. https://apibhs.com/2022/10/03/why-is-being-self-aware-important-for-your-mental-health

Markson, D. (2016, November 6). *Seven Ways to Cultivate Gratitude.* Mindsoother Therapy Center. https://www.mindsoother.com/blog/seven-ways-to-cultivate-gratitude

Mayo Clinic. (2016). *Seasonal affective disorder treatment: Choosing a light therapy box.* Mayo Clinic. https://www.mayoclinic.org/diseases-conditions/seasonal-affective-disorder/in-depth/seasonal-affective-disorder-treatment/art-20048298

Mayo Clinic. (2023, March 18). *Biofeedback - Mayo Clinic.* Mayoclinic.org. https://www.mayoclinic.org/tests-procedures/biofeedback/about/pac-20384664

McCallum, K. (2021, September 13). *Brain Chemistry & Your Mood: 4 Hormones That Promote Happiness.* Www.houstonmethodist.org. https://www.houstonmethodist.org/blog/articles/2021/sep/brain-chemistry-your-mood-4-hormones-that-promote-happiness/

McCarthy, A. (2023, October 31). *Floatation Therapy: I Tried Floating in a Soundproof, Lightproof Tank To Relax.* Health. https://www.health.com/mind-body/floatation-therapy

McDermott, N. (2022, November 9). *How Gratitude Can Transform Your Mental Health.* Forbes Health. https://www.forbes.com/health/mind/mental-health-benefits-of-gratitude/

McGloin, B. (2022, August 30). *7 Simple Ways to Reduce Your Screen Time.*

Knowadays. https://knowadays.com/blog/7-simple-ways-to-reduce-your-screen-time/

McLachlan, S. (2021, December 22). *The Science of Habit: How to Rewire Your Brain.* Healthline. https://www.healthline.com/health/the-science-of-habit

McMaster University. (2021, October 5). *7 Benefits of Spending Time in Nature.* Student Wellness Centre. https://wellness.mcmaster.ca/7-benefits-of-spending-time-in-nature/

McRae, BSc, A. (2022, May 25). *Biofeedback Therapy: What You Need to Know.* Psych Central. https://psychcentral.com/health/biofeedback-therapy#how-to-find-it

Mental Health America. (2023). *How to keep a mental health journal.* MHA Screening. https://screening.mhanational.org/content/how-keep-mental-health-journal/

Mental Health Foundation. (2022, January 25). *Diet and mental health.* Www.mentalhealth.org.uk; mental health foundation . https://www.mentalhealth.org.uk/explore-mental-health/a-z-topics/diet-and-mental-health

Mental Health Foundation. (2023). *Nurturing our relationships during challenging times.* Www.mentalhealth.org.uk. https://www.mentalhealth.org.uk/explore-mental-health/articles/nurturing-our-relationships-during-challenging-times

Milkman, K. (2021, November 29). *How to build a habit in 5 steps, according to science.* CNN. https://edition.cnn.com/2021/11/29/health/5-steps-habit-builder-wellness/index.html

Mind My Peelings. (2020, June 18). *Journaling for Mental Health.* Mind My Peelings. https://www.mindmypeelings.com/blog/journaling-mental-health

Mind my peelings. (2021, February 26). *10 Principles of Cognitive Behavior Therapy.* Mind My Peelings. https://www.mindmypeelings.com/blog/cbt-principles

Mindful Arts Therapy. (2022). *Art Therapy - Success Stories and Case Studies - Mindful Arts Therapy.* Mindfulartstherapy.com.au. https://mindfulartstherapy.com.au/art-therapy-success-stories-and-case-studies/

Mindful Staff. (2019, November 25). *How to practice gratitude.* Mindful. https://www.mindful.org/an-introduction-to-mindful-gratitude/

MindWise Innovations. (2017, July 24). *The Importance of Social Connection.* MindWise. https://www.mindwise.org/blog/uncategorized/the-importance-of-social-connection/

Ministry of Health Singapore. (2023, November 22). *mythsandmisconceptionsaboutdepression.* Www.healthhub.sg. https://www.healthhub.sg/live-healthy/mythsandmisconceptionsaboutdepression

Moran, F. (2023, August 9). *5 Benefits of Taking a Digital Detox.* Dymin Systems. https://www.dyminsystems.com/about/blogs/technology-updates/5-benefits-of-taking-a-digital-detox/

Nast, C. (2023, April 27). *7 Ways to Be More Mindful Without Meditating*. SELF. https://www.self.com/story/best-mindfulness-exercises

National Institute of Mental Health. (2022, December). *Caring for your Mental Health*. National Institute of Mental Health. https://www.nimh.nih.gov/health/topics/caring-for-your-mental-health

National Institutes of Health. (2021, June 1). *Mindfulness for your health*. NIH News in Health. https://newsinhealth.nih.gov/2021/06/mindfulness-your-health

Nemrow, S. (2019, January 17). *How to Overcome Unhealthy Coping Mechanisms*. Shanna Nemrow. https://shannanemrow.com/2019/01/how-to-overcome-unhealthy-coping-mechanisms/

Neurospa Mental Health and Wellness. (2020, August 25). *Depression Triggers: What They Are and How to Cope with Them*. Neurospa Mental Health and Wellness. https://neurospamentalhealth.com/depression-triggers-what-are-they-and-how-to-cope-with-them/

Newman, K. (2016, November 9). *Five science-backed strategies to build resilience*. Greater Good. https://greatergood.berkeley.edu/article/item/five_science_backed_strategies_to_build_resilience

Newport Institute. (2020, October 6). *What Is a Digital Detox and Why Should You Do One?* Newport Institute. https://www.newportinstitute.com/resources/mental-health/digital-detox/

One Yoga. (2023, August 31). *Yoga Nidra: A Step-by-Step Guide to Yogic Sleep for Top Relaxation*. One Yoga. https://oneyogathailand.com/yoga-nidra-step-by-step-guide-to-yogic-sleep-for-top-relaxation/

Onyango, O. (2023, September 23). *The Power of Mindset in Fighting Depression*. Www.linkedin.com. https://www.linkedin.com/pulse/power-mindset-fighting-depression-odero-onyango

Optimum Performance Institute . (2017, July 19). *Finding Joy in the Midst of Depression - Embrace Happiness and Well-being*. OPI. https://www.optimumperformanceinstitute.com/finding-joy-in-the-midst-of-depression/

Pal, P., Hauck, C., Goldstein, E., Bobinet, K., & Bradley, C. (2018, December 13). *5 simple mindfulness practices for daily life*. Mindful. https://www.mindful.org/take-a-mindful-moment-5-simple-practices-for-daily-life/

Parker, S. (2021). The science of habits. *Knowable Magazine | Annual Reviews*, *10.1146/knowable-071521-1*. https://doi.org/10.1146/knowable-071521-1

Parkinson's NSW. (2021, April 5). *Four Happy Hormones | Parkinsons NSW*. Parkinsons NSW. https://www.parkinsonsnsw.org.au/four-happy-hormones/

Pathare, S. (2020, October 12). *Yoga Nidra: How To Practice And Top 5 Health Benefits*. HealthifyMe. https://www.healthifyme.com/blog/yoga-nidra-how-to-practice-and-top-5-health-benefits/

Pedersen, T. (2022, May 6). *7 tips for improving your self-awareness*. Psych Central.

https://psychcentral.com/health/how-to-be-more-self-aware-and-why-its-important

Perry, ACC, E. (2023, October 12). *6 Ways to Embrace Change in Your Life.* Www.betterup.com. https://www.betterup.com/blog/embrace-change

Perry, E. (2022, September 14). *What is self-awareness and how to develop it.* BetterUp. https://www.betterup.com/blog/what-is-self-awareness

Petrocchi, N., & Couyoumdjian, A. (2016). The impact of gratitude on depression and anxiety: the mediating role of criticizing, attacking, and reassuring the self. *Self and Identity*, *15*(2), 191–205. https://doi.org/10.1080/15298868.2015.1095794

Pietrangelo, A. (2022, September 22). *The Effects of Depression in Your Body.* Healthline; Healthline Media. https://www.healthline.com/health/depression/effects-on-body

Platero, A. (2021, November 11). *7 Steps of Habit Formation | Psychology Today.* Www.psychologytoday.com. https://www.psychologytoday.com/us/blog/reflect-and-reset/202111/7-steps-habit-formation

Porter, E. (2013, December 9). *9 Depression Myths.* Healthline; Healthline Media. https://www.healthline.com/health/9-myths-depression

Possing, S., & Reyes, A. (2024, February 18). *How to Be Open-Minded: 12 Changes You Can Make Right Now.* WikiHow. https://www.wikihow.com/Be-Open-Minded

Profound. (2024). *Biofeedback for Depression | Therapy - Profound Treatment.* Profound Treatment. https://profoundtreatment.com/biofeedback-for-depression/

Psychology Today. (2019). *Optimism | Psychology Today.* Psychology Today. https://www.psychologytoday.com/us/basics/optimism

Psychology Today. (2024). *The Science of Happiness | Psychology Today.* Www.psychologytoday.com; Sussex Publishers, LLC . https://www.psychologytoday.com/us/basics/happiness/the-science-happiness

Putnam, L. (2016, July 14). *My dog cured my depression.* New York Post. https://nypost.com/2016/07/14/my-dog-cured-my-depression/

QPS. (2022, April 27). *Novel Approaches to Treating Depression.* QPS. https://www.qps.com/2022/04/27/novel-approaches-to-treating-depression/

Raypole, C. (2019, September 30). *How to Hack Your Hormones for a Better Mood.* Healthline; Healthline Media. https://www.healthline.com/health/happy-hormone

Reeves, J. (2015, February 23). *What is yoga nidra?* Ekhart Yoga. https://www.ekhartyoga.com/articles/practice/what-is-yoga-nidra

Reid, S. (2024, February 5). *Gratitude: The Benefits and How to Practice It - HelpGuide.org.* Https://Www.helpguide.org. https://www.helpguide.org/arti

cles/mental-health/gratitude.htm

Rekhi, S. (2023). *Coping Mechanisms: Definition, Examples, & Types*. The Berkeley Well-Being Institute. https://www.berkeleywellbeing.com/coping-mechanisms.html

Rodriguez, C. I., & Zorumski, C. F. (2023). Rapid and novel treatments in psychiatry: the future is now. *Neuropsychopharmacology*, 1–2. https://doi.org/10.1038/s41386-023-01720-2

Rosen, D. A. (2019, April 17). *The Connection Between Diet And Mental Health*. Center for Treatment of Anxiety & Mood Disorders. https://www.centerforanxietydisorders.com/diet-and-mental-health/

Rosenthal, S. (2024). *11 Tips for Mental Health & Well-being | Columbia University | Child Psychiatry*. Childadolescentpsych.cumc.columbia.edu. https://childadolescentpsych.cumc.columbia.edu/articles/11-tips-mental-health-well-being

Ruiz, R. (2022, January 15). *5 easy ways to start practicing mindfulness now*. Mashable. https://mashable.com/article/mindfulness-exercises-for-beginners

Samvedna. (2023, December 19). *The Importance Of Regular Check-Ins With Your Mental Health Therapist*. Samvedna Care. https://www.samvednacare.com/blog/the-importance-of-regular-check-ins-with-your-mental-health-therapist/

Sawchuk, C. (2022, October 14). *Depression (major depressive disorder)*. Mayo Clinic; Mayo Foundation for Medical Education and Research. https://www.mayoclinic.org/diseases-conditions/depression/symptoms-causes/syc-20356007

Scott, E. (2022, November 14). *What Is optimism?* Verywell Mind. https://www.verywellmind.com/the-benefits-of-optimism-3144811

Scribner, H. (2014, September 23). *9 true stories of overcoming depression*. Deseret News. https://www.deseret.com/2014/9/23/20549095/9-true-stories-of-overcoming-depression

Sears, PT, B. (2012). *Biofeedback Therapy: Control Involuntary Actions in Your Body*. Verywell Health. https://www.verywellhealth.com/biofeedback-therapy-5211371

Seed, S. (2021, November 11). *Foods to Fight Depression*. WebMD. https://www.webmd.com/depression/ss/slideshow-foods-fight-depression

Selhub, E. (2022, September 18). *Nutritional psychiatry: Your brain on food* . Harvard Health Blog; Harvard Health Publishing. https://www.health.harvard.edu/blog/nutritional-psychiatry-your-brain-on-food-201511168626

Sheasby, L. (2023, June 22). *Virtual Reality in Healthcare*. www.theaccessgroup.com. https://www.theaccessgroup.com/en-gb/blog/hsc-virtual-reality-in-healthcare/

Smiling Mind. (2023, July 28). *Journaling for Mental Health: Where do you Start?*

Blog.smilingmind.com.au. https://blog.smilingmind.com.au/how-to-journal-for-mental-health-and-wellbeing

Smith, MA, M., Robinson, L., & Segal, Ph.D. , J. (2019, January 3). *Depression Treatment*. HelpGuide.org. https://www.helpguide.org/articles/depression/depression-treatment.htm

Smith, L. (2015, July 16). *The Importance of Seeking Help for Depression | HealthyPlace*. Www.healthyplace.com. https://www.healthyplace.com/blogs/copingwithdepression/2015/07/the-importance-of-seeking-help-for-depression

Smith, M. (2019, March 12). *Depression Symptoms and Warning Signs*. HelpGuide.org. https://www.helpguide.org/articles/depression/depression-symptoms-and-warning-signs.htm

Solis-Moreira, J. (2023, December 4). *How Depression Affects Your Brain*. Www.psycom.net. https://www.psycom.net/depression/depressed-brain

SonderMind. (2023, July 23). *6 Cognitive Behavioral Therapy Exercises To Try | SonderMind*. Www.sondermind.com. https://www.sondermind.com/resources/articles-and-content/cognitive-behavioral-therapy-exercises/

Spector, N. (2019, November 6). *What is self-awareness? And how can you cultivate it?* NBC News. https://www.nbcnews.com/better/lifestyle/what-self-awareness-how-can-you-cultivate-it-ncna1067721

St. Bonaventure University Online. (2022, January 25). *Strategies for Reframing Negative Thoughts*. Online.sbu.edu. https://online.sbu.edu/news/strategies-reframing-negative-thoughts

Stanborough, R. J. (2020, February 4). *How to change negative thinking with cognitive restructuring*. Healthline. https://www.healthline.com/health/cognitive-restructuring

Steinhilber, B. (2017, August 24). *How to be an optimist, when you always see the negative*. NBC News. https://www.nbcnews.com/better/health/how-train-your-brain-be-more-optimistic-ncna795231

Street, F. (2012, March 25). *The Science Of Habit Formation And Change*. Farnam Street. https://fs.blog/everything-you-need-to-know-about-habits-the-science-of-habit-formation-and-change/

Sutter Health. (2019). *Eating Well for Mental Health | Sutter Health*. Sutterhealth.org. https://www.sutterhealth.org/health/nutrition/eating-well-for-mental-health

Suttie, J. (2017, November 13). *Four Ways Social Support Makes You More Resilient*. Greater Good. https://greatergood.berkeley.edu/article/item/four_ways_social_support_makes_you_more_resilient

Sutton, Ph.D, J. (2018, May 14). *5 Benefits of Journaling for Mental Health*. Positive-Psychology.com. https://positivepsychology.com/benefits-of-journaling/#benefits

Sutton, J. (2020, November 4). *What Is Virtual Reality Therapy? The Future of*

Psychology. PositivePsychology.com. https://positivepsychology.com/virtual-reality-therapy/

Swetha Amaresan. (2018). *10 Creative Ways to Keep a Positive Attitude -- No Matter What*. Hubspot.com. https://blog.hubspot.com/service/positive-attitude

TAPinto Staff. (2022, October 17). *Nurturing a Strong Social Circle for Better Health*. TAPinto. https://www.tapinto.net/towns/princeton/columns/healthy-living/articles/nurturing-a-strong-social-circle-for-better-health

TeamFloat8. (2020, January 30). *What is Floatation Therapy? Here's What to Expect | Float8*. Float8 Wellness Lounge. https://float8ion.com/floating-101/what-is-floatation-therapy/

Test, A. (2017, December 22). *Cultivate Optimism*. Jody Michael Associates. https://www.jodymichael.com/blog/10-ways-to-cultivate-optimism/

The Depression Project. (2023, June 9). *5 Ways To Find Joy When You Are Depressed*. The Depression Project. https://thedepressionproject.com/blogs/news/5-ways-to-find-joy-when-you-are-depressed

The Float Space. (2018, December 19). *Floating For Depression Relief | The Float Space Brisbane*. The Float Space. https://thefloatspace.com.au/floater/floating-for-anxiety-depression/

The Mix. (2019, January 10). *How positive change could improve your mental health*. The Mix. https://www.themix.org.uk/mental-health/how-positive-change-could-improve-your-mental-health-30207.html

The Recovery Village. (2023, May 8). *9 Common Depression Triggers | The Recovery Village*. The Recovery Village Drug and Alcohol Rehab. https://www.therecoveryvillage.com/mental-health/depression/depression-triggers/

Think Mental Health. (2020). *Mental Health Self-Assessment Tool*. Think Mental Health. https://www.thinkmentalhealthwa.com.au/mental-health-self-assessment-checklist/

Thomas, C. (2022, September 14). *16 Best Ways to Reduce Screen Time | ExpressVPN Blog*. Home of Internet Privacy. https://www.expressvpn.com/blog/ways-to-reduce-or-limit-your-screen-time/

Thurrott, S. (2022, October 4). *Getting Help for Symptoms of Depression | Banner Health*. Www.bannerhealth.com. https://www.bannerhealth.com/healthcare blog/better-me/steps-for-seeking-help-for-symptoms-of-depression

Tigar, L. (2023, April 7). *The Benefits of Spending Time in Nature: Why You Should Get Outside More Often*. Real Simple. https://www.realsimple.com/benefits-of-spending-time-in-nature-7376683

Tokitus Team. (2021). *Professional Therapy Online For An Affordable Price | Tokitus*. Tokitus.com. https://tokitus.com/blog/nine-mood-boosting-activities-to-imporove-mental-health

Tracy, B. (2016, April 21). *7 Steps to Developing a New Habit*. Brian Tracy's Self

Improvement & Professional Development Blog. https://www.briantracy.com/blog/personal-success/seven-steps-to-developing-a-new-habit/

Tracy, N. (2023, February 17). *Replace a Negative Coping Skill with a Positive Coping Skill | HealthyPlace*. Www.healthyplace.com. https://www.healthyplace.com/blogs/breakingbipolar/2023/2/replace-a-negative-coping-skill-with-a-positive-coping-skill

Turner, M. (2023, October 27). *8 Common Depression Triggers & How to Cope With Them*. Choosing Therapy. https://www.choosingtherapy.com/depression-triggers/

UnityPoint Health. (2023). *11 Common Myths About Depression*. Www.unitypoint.org. https://www.unitypoint.org/news-and-articles/11-common-myths-about-depression-unitypoint-health

Valentin, A. (2022, February 11). *What Triggers Depression? | Clearbrook Treatment Massachusetts*. Clearbrook Treatment Centers. https://www.clearbrookinc.com/news/what-triggers-depression/

Vallie, S. (2022, August 12). *What to Know About Yoga Nidra*. WebMD. https://www.webmd.com/balance/what-to-know-yoga-nidra

Vanbuskirk, S. (2021, May 29). *What Is Light Therapy and Is It Right For You?* Verywell Mind. https://www.verywellmind.com/what-is-light-therapy-and-is-it-right-for-you-5097392

Vessel Floats. (2023, December 13). *What to do before a Sensory Deprivation Tank*. Vessel Floats. https://www.vesselfloats.com/journal/what-to-do-before-sensory-deprivation-float-tank

Villines, Z. (2023a, August 16). *The effects of depression on the body and physical health*. MedicalNewsToday. https://www.medicalnewstoday.com/articles/322395

Villines, Z. (2023b, October 13). *VR therapy for phobias, depression, PTSD, and more*. Www.medicalnewstoday.com. https://www.medicalnewstoday.com/articles/vr-therapy

Viveros, J., & Schramm, D. (2021, January 11). *Strategies for Dealing with Life's Difficulties*. Extension.usu.edu. https://extension.usu.edu/relationships/research/strategies-for-dealing-with-lifes-difficulties

Vogel, K. (2022, March 10). *Light Therapy Treatment for Depression*. Psych Central. https://psychcentral.com/depression/light-therapy-for-depression

Warley, S. (n.d.). *What Is Self-Awareness?* Life Skills That Matter. Retrieved April 6, 2024, from https://www.lifeskillsthatmatter.com/blog/self-awareness

Watson, S. (2021, July 20). *Feel-good hormones: How they affect your mind, mood and body*. Harvard Health. https://www.health.harvard.edu/mind-and-mood/feel-good-hormones-how-they-affect-your-mind-mood-and-body

Watt, A. (2013, December 10). *Light Therapy and Depression*. Healthline. https://

www.healthline.com/health/depression/light-therapy

Web MD Editorial Contributors. (2022, September 27). *Health Care Providers That Treat Depression*. WebMD. https://www.webmd.com/depression/taking-first-step-healthcare-providers-treating-depression-medref

WebMD. (2012). *Slideshow: Celebrities with Depression*. WebMD. https://www.webmd.com/depression/ss/slideshow-depression-celebs

Weingus, L. (2022a, June 2). *70 Journal Prompts for Depression*. Silk + Sonder. https://www.silkandsonder.com/blogs/news/journal-prompts-for-depression

Weingus, L. (2022b, August 29). *12 Ways to Practice Self-Reflection (and What It Is)*. Silk + Sonder. https://www.silkandsonder.com/blogs/news/self-reflection

Wellness, S., & Prevention. (2018, February 14). *Should Adults Reduce Their Screen Time?* Scripps Health. https://www.scripps.org/news_items/6310-8-tips-to-reduce-screen-time-for-adults

Whelan, C. (2016, November 14). *Is It Depression or Sadness? Learn the Signs*. Healthline; Healthline Media. https://www.healthline.com/health/depression/depression-vs-sadness

Whittaker, G. (2022, August 14). *Depression Checklist: Measuring Your Depression*. Hers. https://www.forhers.com/blog/depression-checklist

Will. (2022, April 21). *The Science Behind How Yoga Nidra Affects Your Mental Health*. MyYogaTeacher. https://myyogateacher.com/articles/yoga-nidra-science

Wilson, S. (2018, October 24). *The 4 Ways Depression Can Physically Affect Your Brain*. Healthline. https://www.healthline.com/health/depression-physical-effects-on-the-brain

Woodland, S. (n.d.). *The Power of Positivity in Battling Depression: Hope Mental Health: Psychiatric Mental Health Specialists*. Www.hopementalhealth.com. Retrieved April 13, 2024, from https://www.hopementalhealth.com/blog/the-power-of-positivity-in-battling-depression

World Health Organization. (2023, March 31). *Depressive Disorder (depression)*. World Health Organization; World Health Organization. https://www.who.int/news-room/fact-sheets/detail/depression

World Health Organization Europe. (2024). *WHO depression self-assessment tool*. Www.who.int. https://www.who.int/europe/tools-and-toolkits/who-depression-self-assessment-tool

World Health Organization Western Pacific. (2021, October 7). *6 ways to take care of your mental health and well-being this World Mental Health Day*. Www.who.int. https://www.who.int/westernpacific/about/how-we-work/pacific-support/news/detail/07-10-2021-6-ways-to-take-care-of-your-mental-health-and-well-being-this-world-mental-health-day

Wright, K. W. (2023, June 28). *8 Benefits of Journaling For Mental Health*. Day One |

Your Journal for Life. https://dayoneapp.com/blog/benefits-of-journaling-for-mental-health/

Young, S. H. (2007, August 14). *18 Tricks to Make New Habits Stick.* Lifehack; Lifehack. https://www.lifehack.org/articles/featured/18-tricks-to-make-new-habits-stick.html

Yu, A. (2021, January 29). *Lumino.* Luminohealth.sunlife.ca. https://luminohealth.sunlife.ca/s/article/The-importance-of-mental-health-check-ins?language=en_US

Zayed, MD, A. (2023, July 10). *10 Principles of Cognitive Behavioral Therapy.* The Diamond Rehab - Drug & Alcohol Rehab in Thailand. https://diamondrehabthailand.com/cognitive-behavioral-therapy-principles/

Made in United States
Orlando, FL
28 September 2024

52062276R00093